*Beanie*Mania

A COMPREHENSIVE
COLLECTOR'S GUIDE

1st Edition

All Rights Reserved

An Unofficial Collector's Guide

Beanie Mania

A COMPREHENSIVE COLLECTOR'S GUIDE

Becky Phillips and Becky Estenssoro

First Edition: July, 1997
Second Printing: September, 1997
Third Printing: October, 1997
Fourth Printing: November, 1997

Library of Congress Card Catalog Number: 97-92285

ISBN 0-9659036-0-5

For information write:

Dinomates, Inc.
710 East Ogden Avenue, Suite 530
Naperville, Illinois 60563

Printed in the United States of America

We dedicate this book to our families who have

given us their love and encouragement; to all

our friends  around the

world who helped make this dream come true,

and to all kids and kids at heart

who love Beanie Babies.

cknowledgments

Our deepest thanks to all who helped in so many ways:

To H. Ty Warner, the creative genius, whose Beanie Babies were the inspiration
behind this book.

To Vicky Krupka, a contributing author and friend, who gave so much of herself
in the creation of this book.

To Sara Nelson (BeanieMom), whose hard work and devotion has created the best
"family" Beanie Baby web site on the Internet.

To George Burns, our photographer, for his amazing talent and hard work;
who sacrificed his time to come to our aid numerous times.

To all of our friends around the world, too numerous to mention,
who helped make this dream come true.

To Robyn Konlon and Kayleen Knipper (cover designer)
of Konlon and Associates.

To Steve Arazmus, cover photographer.

To Kern Hagg and Michael McKellar from Hagg Press, Inc., Elgin Illinois
whose talent and genuine interest helped with the
completion of this project.

Private Collector Acknowledgments

Flutter, the butterfly (prototype) and Coral, the tie-dyed fish (prototype), from the private collection of Jamie Primack.

Lizzy, the lizard with the striped tail, from the private collection of Brian Lister.

Libearty, the American flag bear with the flag upside down, from the private collection of Christopher Estenssoro.

Derby, the brown horse with the ear on backward, from the private collection of Gregory Pitner.

Inky, the pink octopus with the nine legs, from the private collection of Sally Christoffel.

Quackers, the duck with no eyes or eyebrows, from the private collection of Michelle Phillips.

Quackers, the duck with the wing on backwards, from the private collection of Kerri Hanson.

Righty, the elephant with no flag, from the private collection of Michael Sobolewski.

Lefty, the donkey with no flag, from the private collection of Chris Wagner.

Stripes, the tiger with the "fuzzy" belly, from the private collection of Kristen Sobolewski.

Daisy, the black and white cow without spot, from the private collection of Joan Pitner.

Spot, the dog with the white face, from the private collection of Barbara Venier.

Stripes, the tiger with the stripes running lengthwise, from the private collection of Rob Hemingway.

Teenie Beanie prototypes, from the private collection of Stephanie Christoffel.

Teenie Beanie renderings and 3-D logo, from the private collection of Jim Christoffel.

THE ROAD NOT TAKEN
by Robert Frost

Two roads diverged in a yellow wood,
And sorry I could not travel both
And be one traveler, long I stood
And looked down one as far as I could
To where it bent in the undergrowth;

Then took the other, as just as fair,
And having perhaps the better claim,
Because it was grassy and wanted wear;
Though as for that the passing there
Had worn them really about the same,

And both that morning equally lay
In leaves no step had trodden black.
Oh, I kept the first for another day!
Yet knowing how way leads on to way,
I doubted if I should ever come back.

I shall be telling this with a sigh
Somewhere ages and ages hence:
Two roads diverged in a wood, and I--
I took the one less traveled by,
And that has made all the difference.

Table Of Contents

Mr. H. Ty Warner, sole owner of Ty Inc., graduated in 1962 from Kalamazoo College in Kalamazoo, Michigan. He went to work for Dakin, Inc., a San Francisco based manufacturer of stuffed animals. Mr. Warner left Dakin in 1980 and spent the next five years traveling throughout Europe and the Orient.

After his travels, he created his first plush animals, the "Himalayan" cats. They ranged in size from 12 inches to 20 inches long and were priced from $10 to $20.

Smokey Himalayan

Angel Himalayan

Ginger Himalayan

Peaches Himalayan

These Himalayan cats are individually air-brushed by hand. Their eyes are hand painted, and their paws and tush are weighted.

Mr. Warner, who established Ty Inc. in 1986, continued to design a full line of stuffed animals of this size, including a series of "Annual Collectable Bears," which were introduced in 1991. Ty Inc. was a successful international enterprise long before Beanie Babies, opening offices in England (Ty UK), Germany (Ty Deutschland), Mexico (Ty Mexico), and Canada (Ty Canada).

1991 Annual Collectable Bear

1992 Annual Collectable Bear

Mr. Warner eventually came up with the idea to design smaller and less expensive versions of these stuffed animals. He wanted them to be priced low enough so kids could afford to buy them with their allowances, and small enough to be held in the palms of their hands. Soon, the Beanie Babies were born. The first nine Beanie Babies were displayed at a toy exposition in late 1993.

From the beginning, Mr. Warner's marketing strategy for Beanie Babies has been to limit their availability, in order to create a sense of scarcity and stimulate demand. Borrowing from marketing lessons he learned at Dakin, Inc., he avoided the more common marketing plan of selling through the nationally owned mass merchants, such as Wal-Mart and Toys R Us. Instead, Beanie Babies are only sold through small retail stores, such as card shops, specialty gift stores, small toy stores and airport gift shops. Another important part of Ty's strategy to create scarcity and to ensure that the Beanie Babies are not just another short lived fad, has been to periodically discontinue, or "retire," a select number of the Beanie Babies. These "limited editions" have become highly prized by collectors and have helped to heighten the demand for all types of Beanie Babies.

Sales didn't take off right away. It wasn't until the 1995 Christmas season that the adorable little Beanie Babies started to become popular. Sales began to pick up steam in the spring of 1996. Soon, something magical began happening, but only in a few areas. Chicagoland was one of the first hot spots. Children began noticing their friends' new little stuffed toys. They urged their parents to go to the store to buy them a Beanie Baby. They were inexpensive, so people bought several, perhaps one of each type. They became the newest toy to collect. Word spread of their growing popularity. Stories were told of the excitement of the hunt to find stores that sold Beanie Babies, and to find one of each type of Beanie Babies. Adults became curious about why people were waiting in lines to buy these new toys. Soon, the lines were growing longer and stores were selling out truckloads of the Beanie Babies almost as soon as they were delivered. In recent months, Beanie Baby mania has spread to other parts of the United States, as well as into other countries, and this frenzied shopping hunt is being replayed again and again.

Ty expanded to the Internet, opening a web site in August 1996. This provided the opportunity for Beanie Baby lovers from around the world to learn more about the company and its products, as well as exchange information with each other through the "Guestbook." Ty's web site is also used to announce which Beanie Babies are to be retired and to introduce the new designs (more than 100 additional Beanie Babies have been added since the original nine in 1993).

Some entrepreneurial Beanie Baby collectors have started their own web sites, providing not only an information exchange but also a secondary market to find the most sought after Beanie Babies. Now these lovable animals can be bought, sold and traded on-line. Two years ago, most people hadn't even heard of the Internet, let alone Beanie Babies. The nearly simultaneous occurrence of the explosive growth in the use of the Internet and the Beanie Baby becoming the hottest toy in recent memory has created an insatiable worldwide search and demand for Ty Warner's creation.

THE 1993 INTRODUCTIONS:

Brownie, the brown bear
Patti, the deep fuchsia platypus
Punchers, the red lobster

THE 1994 INTRODUCTIONS - ORIGINAL NINE:

Chocolate, the moose
Cubbie, the brown bear
Flash, the dolphin
Legs, the frog
Patti, the raspberry platypus
Pinchers, the red lobster
Splash, the orca whale
Spot, the black and white dog without a spot
Squealer, the pig

THE 1994 MID-YEAR NEW INTRODUCTIONS:

Ally, the alligator
Blackie, the black bear
Bones, the brown dog
Chilly, the white polar bear
Daisy, the black and white cow
Digger, the orange crab
Goldie, the goldfish
Happy, the gray hippo
Humphrey, the camel
Inky, the tan octopus without a mouth
Lucky, the ladybug with 7 felt dots
Mystic, the fine-mane unicorn
Peking, the panda bear
Quacker**s**, the duck with no wings
Seamore, the seal
Slither, the snake
Speedy, the turtle
Teddy, the old face-brown bear
Teddy, the old face-cranberry bear
Teddy, the old face-jade bear
Teddy, the old face-magenta bear
Teddy, the old face-teal bear
Teddy, the old face-violet bear
Trap, the mouse
Web, the spider

OTHER 1994 INTRODUCTIONS:

Quacker, the duck with no wings
Spot, the black and white dog with a spot

THE 1995 INTRODUCTIONS:

Nip, the gold cat with white face and belly
Quacker, the duck with wings
Teddy, the new face-brown bear
Teddy, the new face-cranberry bear
Teddy, the new face-jade bear
Teddy, the new face-magenta bear
Teddy, the new face-teal bear
Teddy, the new face-violet bear
Valentino, the white bear with red heart
Zip, the black cat with white face and belly

OTHER 1995 INTRODUCTIONS:

Bongo, the monkey with brown tail - black and white tush tag
Inky, the tan octopus with a mouth
Nana, the monkey with tan tail - black and white tush tag
Nip, the all gold cat with pink ears (no white)
Patti, the magenta platypus
Quacker**s**, the duck with wings
Spook, the ghost
Zip, the all black cat with pink ears (no white)

THE 1995 MID-YEAR NEW INTRODUCTIONS:

Bessie, the brown and white cow
Bongo, the monkey with tan tail - black and white tush tag
Bronty, the brontosaurus
Bubbles, the black and yellow fish
Caw, the crow
Derby, the fine-mane horse
Digger, the red crab
Flutter, the tie-dyed butterfly
Happy, the lavender hippo
Inky, the pink octopus
Kiwi, the toucan
Lizzy, the tie-dyed lizard
Magic, the white dragon - pink stitching
Peanut, the royal blue elephant
Rex, the tyrannosaurus
Steg, the stegosaurus
Sting, the ray
Stinky, the skunk
Stripes, the black and orange tiger
Tabasco, the red bull
Velvet, the panther
Waddle, the penguin
Ziggy, the zebra

BEANIE BABIES - CHRONOLOGICAL

THE 1996 INTRODUCTIONS:

Bucky, the beaver
Bumble, the bee
Chops, the lamb
Coral, the tie-dyed fish
Derby, the coarse-mane horse
Ears, the brown rabbit
Flip, the white cat
Garcia, the tie-dyed bear
Grunt, the razorback hog
Hoot, the owl
Inch, the inchworm with felt antennae
Lizzy, the blue lizard with black spots
Manny, the manatee
Mystic, the coarse-mane unicorn
Nip, the gold cat with white paws
Patti, the fuchsia platypus
Peanut, the light blue elephant
Pinky, the flamingo
Radar, the bat
Ringo, the raccoon
Seaweed, the otter
Spooky, the ghost
Tank, the 7-line armadillo
Tusk, the walrus
Twigs, the giraffe
Weenie, the dachshund
Zip, the black cat with white paws

THE 1996 MID-YEAR NEW INTRODUCTIONS:

Congo, the gorilla
Curly, the brown napped bear
Freckles, the leopard
Lefty, the donkey with American flag
Libearty/Beanine, the white bear with American flag
Righty, the elephant with American flag
Rover, the red dog
Scoop, the pelican
Scottie, the Scottish terrier
Sly, the brown-belly fox
Sparky, the dalmatian
Spike, the rhinoceros
Wrinkles, the bulldog

OTHER 1996 INTRODUCTIONS:

Bongo, the monkey with brown tail - red tush tag / no name
Bongo, the monkey with tan tail - red tush tag / no name
Bongo, the monkey with tan tail - red tush tag / with name
Inch, the inchworm with yarn antennae
Libearty, the white bear with American flag
Lucky, the ladybug with approx. 11 dots
Lucky, the ladybug with approx. 21 dots
Magic, the white dragon - hot pink stitching
Sly, the white-belly fox
Stripes, the black and tan tiger
Tank, the 9-line armadillo
Tank, the 9-line armadillo with shell
Tu<u>c</u>k, the walrus

THE 1997 INTRODUCTIONS:

Bernie, the St. Bernard
Crunch, the shark
Doby, the doberman
Fleece, the napped lamb
Floppity, the lavender bunny
Gracie, the swan
Hippity, the mint bunny
Hoppity, the rose bunny
Mel, the koala
Nuts, the squirrel
Pouch, the kangaroo
Snip, the Siamese cat
Snort, the red bull with cream paws

OTHER 1997 INTRODUCTIONS:

Bongo, the monkey with brown tail - red tush tag / with name
Maple/Maple, the white bear with Canadian flag
Maple/Pride, the white bear with Canadian flag
Strut, the rooster
Tank, the 7-line armadillo with shell

THE 1997 MID-YEAR NEW INTRODUCTIONS:

Baldy, the eagle
Blizzard, the black and white tiger
Chip, the calico cat
Claude, the tie-dyed crab
Doodle, the rooster
Dotty, the dalmatian
Echo, the dolphin
Jolly, the walrus
Nanook, the husky
Peace, the tie-dyed bear
Pugsly, the pug
Roary, the lion
Tuffy, the terrier
Waves, the orca whale

Flutter – Prototype

Coral – Prototype

During the production process, a Beanie Baby goes through many changes before its final approval. This process can take years of preparation. The design, colors, features, and accessories, as well as the name, poem and type of tags, require a monumental amount of thought, time and effort.

When Ty Warner designs a Beanie Baby, he makes several prototypes of the same Beanie Baby. He designs them in different shapes and colors, and uses a variety of features and accessories. He then calls upon his friends and employees to help make the final selection. He is extremely interested in their opinions and even has them help with the name selection.

Because of Ty Warner's strong desire for perfection, Beanie Babies are in a constant state of change. The most noticeable changes are color variations and redesigns. There are changes made during the photo shoot, after the catalogs and mid-year "New Introduction" sheets are distributed, and for some, during the years that followed.

The Beanie Babies that are pictured in the catalogs and mid-year "New Introduction" sheets are prototypes. The majority of the prototypes pictured were produced as Beanie Babies, but there are several prototypes pictured that did not make the "final cut."

Punchers   *Punchers - prototype*

The Beanie Babies Collection
Punchers ™· Style 4026
TY (UK) LTD. P.O. BOX 18 WATERLOOVILLE
HANTS PO8 9RF
REMOVE TAG/RIBBON BEFORE
GIVING TO A CHILD.
FOR AGES 3 & UP.
RETAIN TAG FOR
REFERENCE.
CE

A notable prototype that is pictured is Punchers. The 1994 catalog lists Pinchers as the red lobster, but the lobster shown in the catalog was a prototype named Punchers. This Punchers prototype is a red lobster with black eyes and black felt twisted whiskers that project from the top of his mouth. His claws are filled with stuffing, making them look like punching bags. His tail segments are evenly spaced and his mouth has a flat appearance.

In 1993, Punchers underwent a design change. The stuffing was taken out of his claws and instead of felt whiskers, two string whiskers (feelers) were attached to the top of his mouth. These rare Punchers have the first version heart tag that reads, "Punchers™ Style 4026". Punchers has a 1993 black and white tush tag and was made in Korea.

In 1994, Punchers' name was changed to Pinchers. There was another slight design change. The two center tail segments were sewn closer together making the outer segments larger.

One of the more unusual prototypes pictured was Nana, the red monkey. In the 1995 mid-year "New Introduction" sheet, Nana is a red-colored monkey with a cream face, hands and feet. Before Nana was introduced in 1995, its color was changed to medium-brown. Also pictured is Stripes, the tiger, with stripes only visible on his face; Sting, the ray, with a white belly and Lizzy, the tie-dyed lizard, with a white belly.*

*See page 117.
See page 134 – Dinosaur prototypes.

In 1993, Ty produced the "Original Nine" Beanie Babies: (top to bottom, left to right) Legs, Chocolate, Flash, Patti, Cubbie, Splash, Pinchers, Squealer and Spot. These nine original Beanie Babies are the "heart" and soul of this collection.

(top row) Raspberry and Magenta
(bottom row) Deep Fuchsia and Fuchsia

Patti, the platypus, was one of the "Original Nine" Beanie Babies that were introduced in 1994. She lays flat on her belly and four yellowish-gold webbed feet full of stuffing, protrude from the sides of her body. Her black eyes peer up at you, and her yellowish-gold stuffed bill juts out waiting for a squeeze. She comes in four colors: deep fuchsia, raspberry, magenta, and fuchsia. Patti's color is a good indicator as to when she was produced. When she was produced in 1993, she was a deep fuchsia color. This Patti was produced in Korea and has the first version heart tag and the black and white tush tag. Before she was introduced in 1994, her color was changed to more of a raspberry color with a burgundy overtone. The majority of these have the first and second version heart tags and were made in Korea. They appear smaller in size because there is less stuffing in them, and their bills have more of a rounded look. The third version Patti is more of a magenta color with a red overtone. The majority of these have the third version heart tag and were made in China. The fourth version is the same fuchsia color that is found on Inch's tail.

The Beanie Babies Collection
Brownie ™· Style 4010
TY (UK) LTD. P.O. BOX 18 WATERLOOVILLE
HANTS. PO8 9RF
REMOVE TAG/RIBBON BEFORE
GIVING TO A CHILD.
FOR AGES 3 & UP.
RETAIN TAG FOR
REFERENCE.
CE

Brownie, the brown bear, was produced in Korea in 1993. Brownie is a medium-brown colored bear with a lighter colored snout. He has black eyes and a brown triangular nose. In 1993, there was a name change and Brownie was changed to Cubbie before the "Original Nine" were introduced in 1994. Brownie has the first version heart tag and "Brownie™ Style 4010" is inscribed on the back of the tag. The only way to distinguish Brownie from the original Cubbie is by the name that is printed on the single heart tag that is attached to the ear.

Quackers the Duck

Quackers, the duck, was introduced in mid-1994. When Quackers was first made, he didn't have any wings. Although a novice flyer, Quackers soon earned his wings, which were given to him in 1995. Quackers was also given wings for stability and balance. Without his wings, Quackers has a tendency to fall to one side as his bill droops into his chest. He has black eyes and black string eyebrows. His bright yellow body rests on orange, oversized webbed feet, and his orange bill sticks out just waiting for a squeeze. This wingless duck also has the 2nd version heart tag with the name "Quacker" printed on it. Before this spelling error was corrected, some of these Quacker tags were also attached to the duck with wings.

The Beanie Babies Collection
Quackers ™ Style 4024
© 1993 Ty Inc. Oakbrook, IL USA
All Rights Reserved. Caution:
Remove this tag before giving
toy to a child. For ages 5 and up
Handmade in China
Surface
Wash.

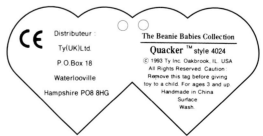

CE Distributeur :
Ty(UK)Ltd.
P.O.Box 18
Waterlooville
Hampshire PO8 8HG

The Beanie Babies Collection
Quacker ™ style 4024
© 1993 Ty Inc. Oakbrook, IL USA
All Rights Reserved. Caution:
Remove this tag before giving
toy to a child. For ages 3 and up
Handmade in China
Surface
Wash.

Spot, the black and white dog, was one of the "Original Nine" Beanie Babies that were introduced in 1994. Spot is a white dog with a black tail, ears and a patch that extends from his left eye to his neck. He has black eyes and a small black nose. When Spot was first produced in 1993, he was designed without a black spot on his back. He was redesigned during the latter part of 1994. To complement his name, a black spot was sewn into the left side of his back.

Chilly, the polar bear, was introduced in mid-1994. He is a smooth, velvety-white bear with black eyes and a triangular black nose. Chilly was retired in 1995.

Peking, the panda bear, was introduced in mid-1994. He has a white body with black legs, shoulders, arms, and tail. Peking is made of smooth velvety material. He has a black triangular nose, and black felt patches attached underneath his eyes complete his panda look. Peking was retired in 1995.

Cubbie, Peking, Chilly and Blackie

Cubbie, Peking, Chilly and Blackie, are the bear quadruplets. The body design of these four bears is the same. With a few facial additions and color changes, Ty was able to add four different bears to a growing list of Beanie Babies.

Peking and Chilly

Cubbie, Peking, Chilly and Blackie

Happy, the gray hippo, was introduced in mid-1994. Happy has tiny black eyes, small rounded ears and soft velvety gray fur. His head is fully stuffed, and his body is filled with a mix of pellets and stuffing. Happy went through a color change and was replaced with Happy, the lavender hippo, who was introduced in mid-1995.

Happy the gray hippo and Happy the lavender hippo

Digger the Crab

Digger, the orange crab, was introduced in mid-1994. He has eight legs and two pincer claws. His black eyes are set close together and two black string feelers (whiskers) protrude from his face and droop below his mouth. Digger went through a color change, and was replaced with Digger, the red crab, in mid-1995. Digger, the red crab, was "officially" retired on May 11, 1997, when Claude, the tie-dyed crab, was introduced.

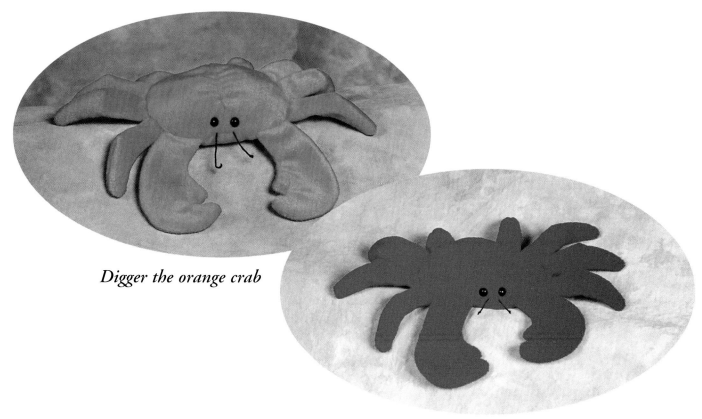

Digger the orange crab

Digger the red crab

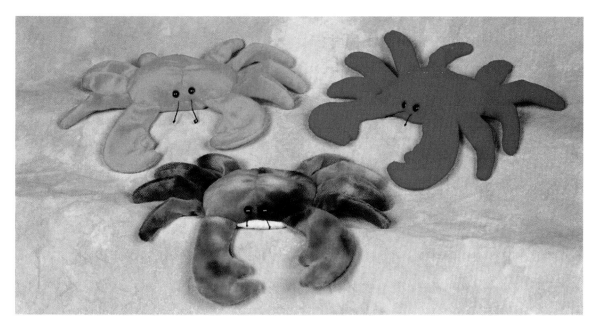

Digger the orange crab, Digger the red crab and Claude the tie-dyed crab

Lucky the Ladybug

Lucky, the ladybug, was introduced in mid-1994. She has seven "Lucky" felt, glued-on dots. Her head, eyes and knotted thread antennae are black. She rests on her black belly with six black felt legs protruding from her sides. It is extremely "Lucky" to find the original ladybug with all seven dots. Many have lost their dots due to poor handling and the glue turning brittle over time. During the latter part of 1996, Ty introduced the ladybug with approximately 11 "Lucky" dots. These dots were no longer glued on, but were part of the fabric. This ladybug has the fourth version heart tag with the yellow star that reads "BEANIE ORIGINAL BABY". It was during this time that Lucky was finally given a May 1, 1995 birthday. A third version of the Ladybug was introduced a few months later. This time Lucky was even luckier with approximately 21 smaller dots.

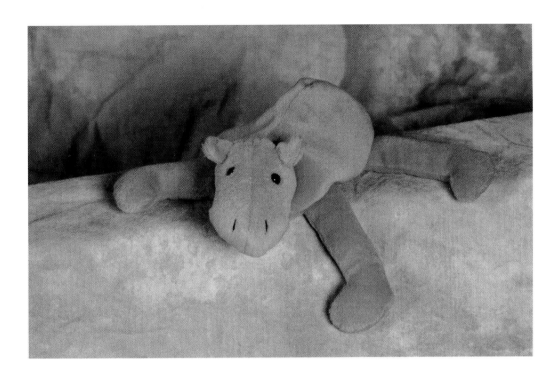

Humphrey, the camel, was introduced in mid-1994. He is a deep-tan color with black eyes and thread nostrils. His tiny ears, which are on the side of his head, seem to frame his cute, wrinkled face. He has one hump that protrudes from the top of his back and a long knotted tail. He seems to be more comfortable resting on his belly with his limp legs sprawled out to his side or underneath him in a sitting position. He was retired in 1995.

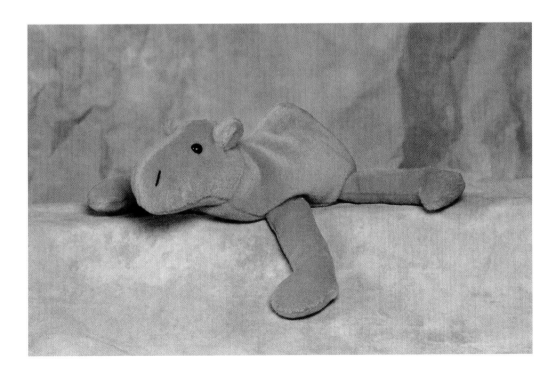

Web, the spider, was introduced in mid-1994. He is a soft velvety black spider with black eyes. He rests on his bright red belly and eight elongated legs. A seam runs from the tip of each leg to midway up the leg, giving his legs a jointed appearance. He looks as if he is ready to dart off. Web was retired in 1995.

Trap, the mouse, was introduced in mid-1994. He is a small gray mouse, with four pink legs protruding from the sides of his body. He has pink ears, a pink nose, and a knotted tail. He has small black eyes that peer up when held in the palm of the hand. His black thread whiskers are flung across his face and are in constant need of straightening. Trap the mouse was retired in 1995.

Inky, the octopus, was introduced in mid-1994. Inky is a tan octopus with black and white oval eyes. His large head is filled with pellets and stuffing and eight tentacles swoop below his body. When Inky was first produced, he did not have a mouth. The 1994 "New Introductions" sheet pictures Inky with a mouth, but the mouth appears to have been drawn onto the picture at a later time.* This explains why most Inkys, without the mouth, have the first and second version heart tags. Inky's mouth, which is "V" shaped, was later sewn on. Inky went through a color change, and in mid-1995, he was replaced with Inky, the pink octopus.

See page 116.

Kiwi, the toucan, was introduced in mid-1995. Kiwi is a brightly colored black, red, yellow and blue bird. He perches majestically on royal blue feet. When held in your hand, his black eyes peer up at you as his oversized bill droops down toward his body. Kiwi was "officially" retired on January 1, 1997.

Caw, the crow, was introduced in mid-1995. Caw is a velvety black crow that is perched on his orange feet. He has black eyes and an orange beak. His black wings blend in with the rest of his body making them look inconspicuous. He was retired in 1996.

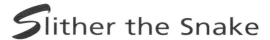

Slither the Snake

Slither, the snake, was introduced in mid-1994. He has a long elegant body that measures approximately 23 inches. He is green on top with brown spots splattered from head to tail. His bright yellow belly adds to his striking appearance. He has little black eyes, and protruding from his mouth is a red felt forked tongue. Slither is definitely one of the rain forest reptiles. If you hold Slither's head and tail in your hands and move him from top to bottom, he will produce the sound of rain for your enjoyment. Slither was retired in 1995.

Derby the Horse

Derby, the horse, was introduced in mid-1995. Derby is a light brown horse with a darker brown mane and tail. He has two-tone ears, and his eyes and thread nostrils are black. Derby was redesigned, and in 1996, larger pieces of yarn were used for his mane and tail.

Note: To determine if you have a fine-mane Derby, count the number of pieces of yarn used for his tail. The fine-mane Derby has approximately 20 pieces of yarn, but the coarse-mane Derby that was introduced in 1996 has approximately eight larger pieces of yarn for a tail.

Mystic the Unicorn

Mystic, the unicorn, was introduced in mid-1994. She is a white unicorn, with a tail and mane made out of thin pieces of white yarn. She has black nostrils, blue eyes, and a tan horn that protrudes from the top of her head. There is an aura of mystery that surrounds Mystic. There have been reports that Mystic was once produced with a horn made out of the same shiny material that is used for Magic's wings. Others say that they have seen Mystic with a horn made of a shiny gold material. Was the horn always tan or were there other earlier variations? Are these variations as mythical as the unicorn, or do they really exist? Could these variations be prototypes, and only a few exist? We hope that these questions will one day be answered, but until that time, the mystery continues. Mystic, the fine-mane unicorn was redesigned, and in 1996, larger pieces of yarn were used for the mane and tail.

Note: To determine if you have a fine-mane Mystic, count the number of pieces of yarn used for the tail. The fine-mane Mystic has approximately 20 pieces of yarn, but the coarse-mane Mystic that was introduced in 1996 has approximately eight larger pieces of yarn for a tail.

Teddy the "Old Face" Bears

(top row) Jade, Cranberry and Violet
(bottom row) Magenta, Brown and Teal

In mid-1994, six "old face" bears were introduced. These bears have thin faces and elongated bodies (no ribbon around the neck). They have black eyes set outside the "V" seam on the face, and a small black triangular nose that is situated on the bottom of the "V" seam. They come in the following colors: jade, cranberry, violet, magenta, brown and teal. There are shade variations between the same color bears. These shade variations are because of the different fabric dye lots that were available in Korea and China where they were produced. These "old face" bears were retired in 1994, the same year they were introduced.

Teddy the "New Face" Bears

(top row) Jade, Cranberry and Violet
(bottom row) Magenta, Brown and Teal

In 1995, six new colored bears were introduced. Although, they were still called Teddy and the colors and style numbers were the same, there was definitely a different look about them. There was a transformation from the "old world" bears to the "new world" bears. The body is fuller and the head is larger and more rounded. The nose is now larger and oval shaped. The ears have increased in size and protrude from the top of the head. Their black eyes are spaced closer together and within the "V" seam of the face.

The different colored ribbons tied in a bow add an accent to the uniform color. Teddy Cranberry and Teddy Violet have green ribbons tied around their necks; Teddy Jade and Teddy Brown (not retired) have a burgandy-colored ribbon; Teddy Magenta has a pink ribbon; and Teddy Teal has a blue ribbon. Different shades can be found between bears of the same color. These shade variations are because of the different fabric dye lots that were available in Korea and China where they were produced. These bears, except for Teddy Brown, were retired in 1995.

Nip the gold cat with the white face and belly

Nip, the gold cat, was introduced in 1995. Her face and body are larger than the Nip that is available today. Her belly and the triangular shape on her face are white. She has a pink triangular nose and solid black eyes. Her triangular pink ears stick straight up and are not curved like later versions. Her mouth and whiskers are a light pink, as compared to the first Nips that were produced with a brighter pink color.

Nip the all gold cat

Nip, the gold cat, went through a design change in mid-1995. The head was made smaller and the width of her body thinner. Her arms were drawn closer into her body to give support to her head. Her pink ears curve inward and the tips are rounded. Her pink mouth is smaller and complements her pink nose and whiskers. Her body and head are now completely gold. Her eyes are black with a gold outer rim. Her reign was short and she was retired at the end of 1995. She was replaced with Nip, the gold cat with white paws, ears and whiskers.

Nip all gold, Nip with white face and belly and Nip with white paws

Zip the black cat with the white face and belly

Zip, the black cat, was introduced in 1995. His face and body are larger than the Zip that is available today. His belly and the triangular shape on his face are white. He has a pink triangular nose and solid black eyes. His triangular pink ears stick straight up and are not curved like the later versions. His mouth and whiskers are a light pink, as compared to the first Zips that were produced with a brighter pink color.

Zip the all black cat

Zip, the black cat, went through a design change in mid-1995. The head was made smaller and the width of his body thinner. His arms were drawn closer into his body to give support to his head. His pink ears curve inward and the tips are rounded. His pink mouth is smaller and complements his pink nose and whiskers. His body and head are now completely black. His eyes are black with a green outer rim. His reign was short and he was retired at the end of 1995. He was replaced with Zip, the black cat with white paws, ears and whiskers.

Zip all black, Zip with white face and belly and Zip with white paws

$\mathcal{F}$lutter the Butterfly

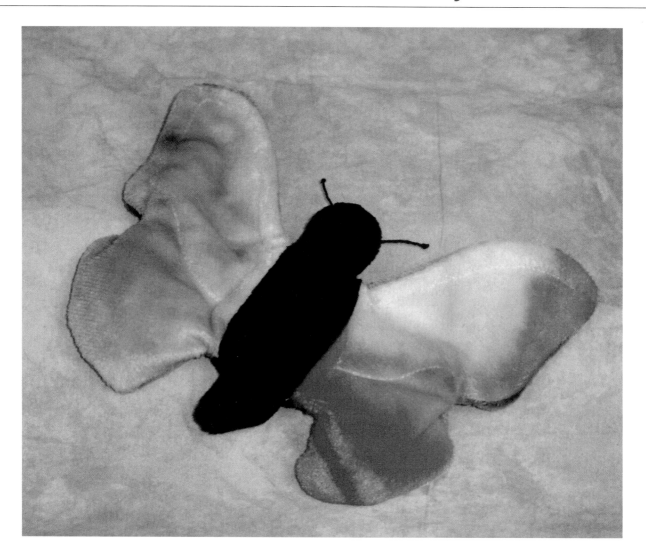

Flutter, the butterfly, was introduced in mid-1995. His black body, as well as the lower portion of his beautiful tie-dyed wings, are filled with pellets and stuffing. He has two black antennae and two knotted pieces of string for eyes. You can't see them—but just feel—they are there! Flutter was retired in the early part of 1996.

Lizzy the Lizard

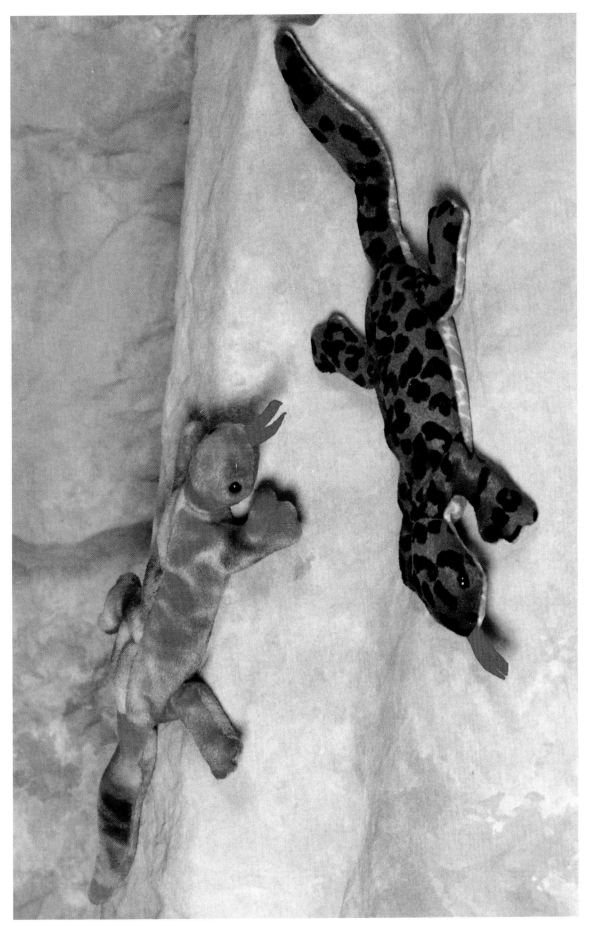

Lizzy, the tie-dyed lizard, was introduced in mid-1995. Lizzy is made up of a wide range of colors. She has an elongated body with little black eyes, four appendages, and a long tail. Protruding from her mouth is a forked tongue made of red felt. Her reign was short and she was retired during the latter part of 1995. She was replaced in 1996 by the blue and black Lizzy with the yellow and orange belly.

Stripes the Tiger

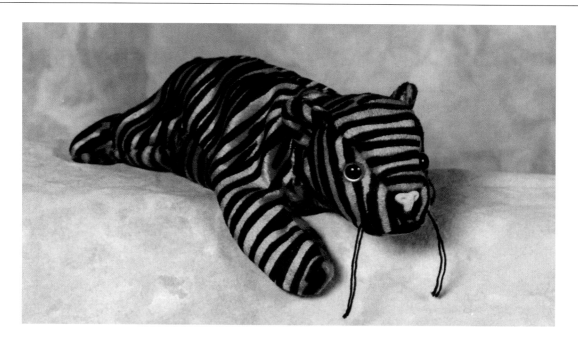

Stripes, the tiger, was introduced in mid-1995. Stripes is an orangish-brown tiger with closely aligned black stripes. His eyes are black with a brown outer rim. He has a velvety flesh-tone nose and two black string whiskers that droop from each side of his mouth. Stripes was redesigned during the latter part of 1996. He was replaced with the current Stripes that is a yellowish-tan color with black stripes that are spaced further apart. Stripes is in great demand because of his scarcity and striking appearance. Blizzard, the black and white tiger, was introduced on May 11, 1997, the newest addition to the tiger family.

Stripes the black and orange tiger, Stripes the black and tan tiger and
Blizzard the black and white tiger

Peanut the Elephant

Peanut, the royal blue elephant, was introduced in mid-1995. Peanut has black eyes and oversized pink and blue ears. She is most comfortable lying on her belly with her hands nestled under her chin. Rumor has it that the original Peanut was supposed to be a light-blue color, but because of a communication error, he was produced with a royal blue color instead. When the mistake was discovered, Peanut was changed to the light-blue elephant that was later introduced in 1996.

Bronty, Rex, and Steg, the dinosaur trio, were first introduced in mid-1995. Because of their tie-dyed fabric, no two are alike. They also vary in shape. They range from a limp to a plump appearance depending on the amount of pellets and stuffing they have inside. Because of the fascination with dinosaurs, they were a great addition to the growing list of Beanie Babies. They became extinct, that is, retired, during the early part of 1996.

Bronty, Rex and Steg

Bronty, the brontosaurus, is a bluish tie-dyed dinosaur with shades of gray and aqua. He walks on all four legs and his black eyes peer up at you. Rumor has it that there were production problems with him because he kept splitting at the seams. Therefore, fewer of him were produced. Because of his scarcity and popularity, he is the most sought after of all three dinosaurs.

Rex, the tyrannosaurus rex, is a pinkish tie-dyed dinosaur with shades of blue, green, burgundy, violet, gray, and brown. He sits on his back legs with his arms extended forward. His black eyes appear smaller because they are set deep in his face.

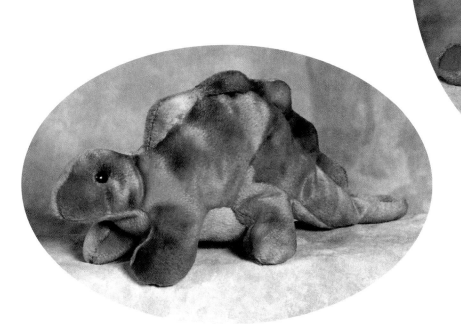

Steg, the stegosaurus, is a brownish-green tie-dyed dinosaur with shades of yellow. Unlike Bronty and Rex, who range from being limp to plump, he has the most consistent full-form of all the dinosaurs. He has larger black eyes and rounded spikes that run the length of his back and tail.

Bumble, the bee, was introduced in 1996. He is a black and yellow striped bee. He has two black antennae that are knotted at the top, and little black eyes. He rests on his six tiny legs and is ready to take flight with his oversized wings. Because he was still in existence in mid-1996, when the fourth version heart tag with the yellow star with "BEANIE ORIGINAL BABY" was introduced, he was given the birth date of October 16, 1995. Bumble was retired in 1996.

Tusk the Walrus

Tusk, the walrus, was introduced in 1996. Tusk is a medium-brown walrus with black eyes and a large black oval nose. Protruding from his mouth are white felt tusks. Depending on how the tusks were attached to the mouth, they will either point forward and up, or point down and back. During the latter part of 1996, Tusk was misspelled "Tuck" on the Ty heart tag. Because mistakes were seldom made prior to January 1, 1997, this "Tuck" Beanie Baby is highly sought after. Tusk was "officially" retired on January 1, 1997, and Jolly, the walrus, was introduced on May 11, 1997, to take his place.

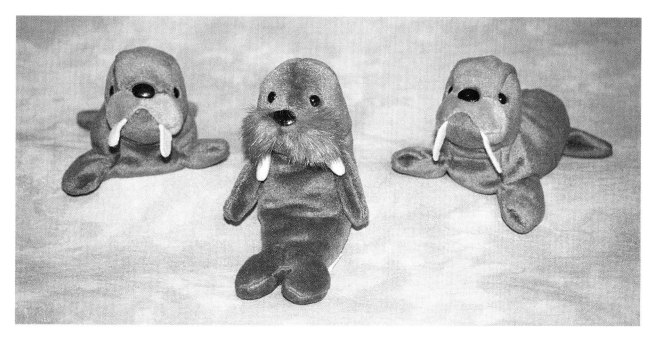

Tusk the walrus (tusks facing forward), Tusk the walrus (tusks facing down)
and Jolly the walrus

Tank the Armadillo

Tank, the armadillo, was introduced in 1996. Tank is a gray armadillo with black eyes and black thread nostrils. His ears are placed on the side of his head outside the "V" stitching on his face. He has 7-lines of stitching on his back to represent a shell. In mid-1996, Tank was redesigned. His color was a shade lighter and two more lines of stitching were added so that his shell now consisted of 9-lines.

During the latter part of 1996, Tank was redesigned again. He still had nine lines sewn on his back, but an additional line was sewn on each side of his body to make the shell look more realistic. His ears were shifted to the top of his head, and his black nostrils were eliminated. His body was approximately two inches shorter. The top of his shell is curved, and a seam is sewn on his belly to draw his frame upward. This Tank is also found with seven lines of stitching.

Inch the Inchworm

Inch, the inchworm, with felt antennae, was introduced in 1996. His multi-colored segments consist of yellow, orange, green, royal blue and fuchsia. He has black eyes and his rounded felt antennae protrude from the top of his head. Because of the way he was designed, he appears to be in constant motion. When Inch was redesigned in 1996, his felt antennae were replaced by yarn antennae. These antennae consist of three pieces of yarn wrapped tightly around each other with the ends tied in a knot.

Sly the Brown-Belly Fox

Sly, the brown-belly fox, was introduced in mid-1996. He is a medium brown fox with a white chin and two-tone ears. He has black eyes, a triangular nose, and two string whiskers project from each side of his mouth. His reign was short. He was redesigned, and Sly, the white-belly fox, took his place during the latter part of 1996.

Bongo the Monkey

Bongo, the monkey, was first introduced in 1995 and was called Nana, the monkey. We assume that Nana was short for "baNana." Nana is a medium-brown monkey with a tan tail, face, ears, hands and feet. He has black eyes and a "V" stitched, thread nose. He has a 1995 black and white tush tag and printed on his heart tag is, "Nana™ Style 4067". In 1995, Nana's name was changed to Bongo. When Bongo was first introduced, he looked exactly like Nana. As time went on though, his tail color changed from tan to brown several times.

Here is a list of the different monkeys:

Nana, with a tan tail and a black and white 1995 tush tag
Bongo, with a tan tail and a black and white 1995 tush tag
Bongo, with a brown tail and a black and white 1995 tush tag
Bongo, with a brown tail and a red and white 1995 tush tag with no name
Bongo, with a tan tail and a red and white 1995 tush tag with no name
Bongo, with a tan tail and a red and white 1995 tush tag with a name
Bongo, with a brown tail and a red and white 1995 tush tag with a name

Pictured in the 1995 mid-year "New Introduction" sheet is a Nana prototype.
Nana is pictured as a red monkey with a cream colored face, hands and feet. See Page 117.

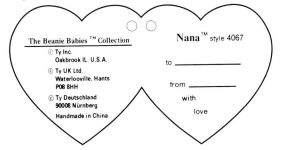

Lefty the Donkey

Lefty, the donkey, was introduced in mid-1996. Lefty is a grayish blue donkey with a black muzzle, and black hooves. He has black eyes, two-tone ears and a black mane and tail made out of yarn. His birthday, July 4th (America's Independence Day), is represented by the American flag that he proudly wears on the left side of his body. He was introduced the same year as the Presidential election and was given the name Lefty to honor the Democratic Party. Lefty was "officially" retired on January 1, 1997.

Righty the Elephant

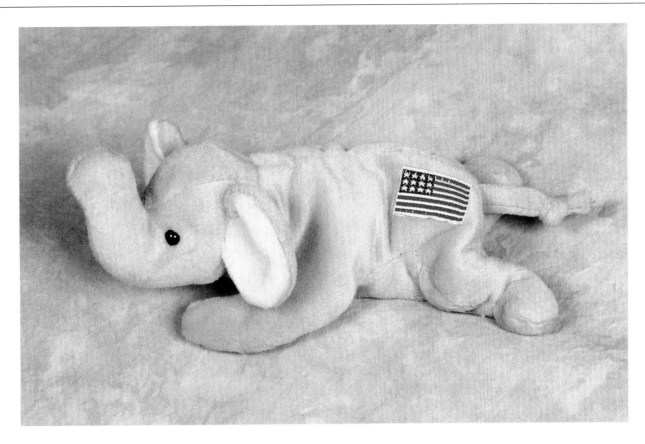

Righty, the elephant, was introduced in mid-1996. Righty is a gray elephant, with black eyes and oversized pink and gray ears. His birthday, July 4th (America's Independence Day), is represented by the American flag that he proudly wears on the left side of his body. He was introduced the same year as the 1996 Presidential election, and was given the name Righty to represent the Republican Party. During his short reign, Righty was never "politically correct." He should have worn the flag on his right hip, but none were ever produced this way. Ty Warner must have intended it to be on the right side, because the 1996 mid-year "New Introduction" sheet* shows the flag placed there, but not attached. Maybe there never was a "correct" prototype? Righty was "officially" retired on January 1, 1997.

The Democratic donkey and the Republican elephant were introduced more than a century ago. The first cartoon picturing the Democratic Party as a donkey appeared in 1837, with the outgoing President Andrew Jackson riding the donkey. Credit for popularizing the Democratic animal goes to cartoonist Thomas Nast. The Republican elephant, also a Thomas Nast creation, was published in 1874. This cartoon appeared In *Harper's Weekly* showing a donkey clad in a lion's skin marked "Caesarism" scaring other beast--including an elephant labeled "The Republican Vote." The elephant quickly emerged as the Republican symbol.

*See page 118.

Libearty, the bear, was introduced in the summer of 1996 in honor of the Summer Olympic games held in Atlanta, Georgia. He wears the American flag proudly on his chest. He is **WHITE** with **RED** and **BLUE** ribbons tied around his neck. He has a brown oval nose and black eyes. When Libearty was first released the word Beanie was misspelled "Beanine" on his tush tag. This Beanine mistake is highly sought after. Libearty was "officially" retired on January 1, 1997.

The American flag consists of red and white stripes that represent the 13 original states, and the stars represent each of the 50 states. White is for purity and innocence. Red is for hardiness and valor. Blue is for vigilance, perseverance, and justice.

Maple, the bear, was introduced in February of 1997, to celebrate Canada's Independence Day on July 1st. He wears the Canadian flag proudly on his chest. He is a **WHITE** bear with a **RED** ribbon tied around his neck. He has a brown oval nose and black eyes.

Maple was originally named Pride, but underwent a name change before being introduced to the public. Approximately 3,000 were produced with the "Pride" tush tag, and the Maple swing tag.

The maple leaf is a national symbol of Canada. The red commemorates the blood shed by Canadians during World War I (1914-1918) and the white represents snow.

Tabasco, the bull, was introduced in mid-1995. He is a red bull with cream colored horns, two-tone ears, black eyes, and black nostrils that are sewn onto his cream colored snout. His poem alludes to the fact that he was introduced to pay homage to the Chicago Bulls, Ty Warner's home basketball team. Rumor has it that he was retired because of a lawsuit that was filed by the company that owns the copyright to the Tabasco Sauce name. Tabasco was "officially" retired on January 1, 1997, when Snort, the bull with the cream colored paws, was introduced to take his place.

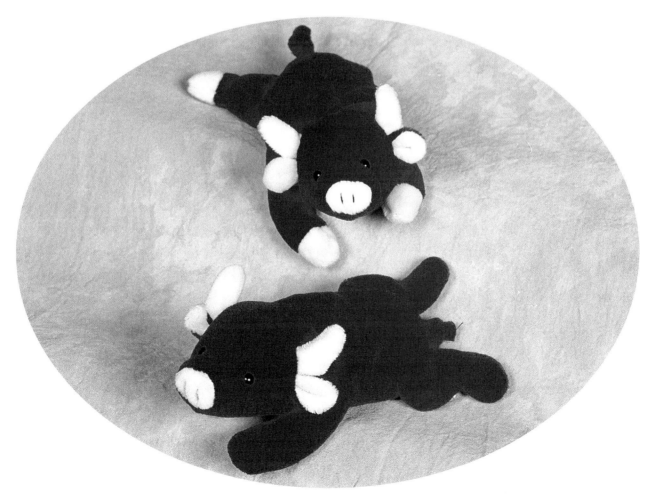

*F*lash the Dolphin

Flash, the dolphin, was one of the "Original Nine" Beanie Babies that was introduced in 1994. He has black eyes, a gray top side and white-belly. He has a beak-like snout, horizontal tail flukes, flippers and a dorsal fin. Flash was "officially" retired on May 11, 1997, and Echo, the dolphin, was introduced to take his place.

Echo and Flash

"Bebe," the last of seven bottlenose dolphins to star in the popular '60s TV series "Flipper" died on May 1, 1997, at the Miami Seaquarium. The 40-year old dolphin gave birth to her eighth calf, "Echo," in 1996.

Splash the Whale

Splash, the whale, was one of the "Original Nine" Beanie Babies that was introduced in 1994. He has black eyes; his top side is black and his under side is white. He has black paddle-shaped flippers, horizontal tail flukes and a dorsal fin. Splash was "officially" retired on May 11, 1997, when Waves the whale was introduced.

Splash and Waves

Grunt, the razorback, was introduced in 1996. He is a red razorback hog with black eyes, thread eyebrows and thread nostrils sewn onto his red snout. White felt tusks flare up from each side of his mouth. He has small, pointed red ears, and razor-like felt spikes that protrude from his back and extend the length of his body. Grunt was "officially" retired on May 11, 1997.

Manny, the manatee, was introduced in 1996. He is a gray manatee with black eyes and thread nostrils. His gray body tapers to a horizontal, flattened tail. The forelimbs are flippers set close to the head. His head is small with a straight snout and a cleft upper lip. Manny was "officially" retired on May 11, 1997.

Note: Manatee is a common name for three species of large water mammals popularly called sea cows.

Coral, Bubbles and Goldie

Coral, Bubbles and Goldie

Coral, the tie-dyed fish, was introduced in 1996. He is the third in a series of fish, with Goldie (introduced in mid-1994) and Bubbles (introduced in mid-1995) preceding him. He is a very bright multi-colored tie-dyed fish. He has black eyes, a puckered mouth, and two over-sized pectoral fins that protrude from the sides of his body. He has a large dorsal fin and tail. He was the first of the fish series to be "officially" retired on January 1, 1997.

Bubbles, the black and yellow fish, was introduced in mid-1995. He is a black and yellow striped fish with an oval shaped body. He has black eyes, a yellow dorsal fin and a yellow tail. Two, large yellow pectoral fins protrude from the sides of his body. Bubbles was "officially" retired on May 11, 1997.

Radar, the bat, was introduced in 1996. He is a black bat with two-tone ears, red eyes and a black triangular shaped nose. He has webbed feet that are made of black felt and a thumb that projects from the top side of each wing. To make it appear as if he is flapping his wings, a pleat was sewn on the under side of each wing. Radar was "officially" retired on May 11, 1997.

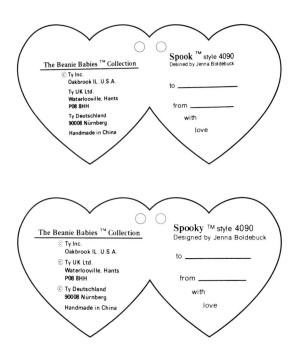

Spook, the ghost, was first produced in 1995 and designed by Jenna Boldebuck. Spook is a white ghost with black oval eyes. He has a "V" shaped grin and a red, crescent mouth. His black grin comes in different shapes depending on how it was sewn on. Around his neck, he has a bright orange ribbon tied in a bow. Prior to his 1996 introduction, Spook's name was changed to Spook**y**. Spook was first produced with a third version heart tag and a black and white 1995 tush tag. We have also seen rare versions of Spooky with a third version heart tag and a black and white tush tag, and Spooky with a third version heart tag with the red and white (no name) tush tag.

Sparky the Dalmatian

Sparky, the dalmatian, was introduced in mid-1996. He is a white dog with black spots splattered from head to tail. He has black eyes, a black triangular nose, and a black sewn in mouth. He was retired because "Sparky" is the registered trademark of the National Fire Protection Association, and Sparky is also the name of the N.F.P.A.'s mascot. He was "officially" retired on May 11, 1997, and was replaced with Dotty, the dalmatian, who has black ears and a black tail.

Dotty and Sparky

Garcia and Peace, the tie-dyed bears

Garcia, the tie-dyed bear, was introduced in 1996. Garcia is a tie-dyed bear with black eyes and a large black oval nose. Because Garcia is tie-dyed, no two are alike. His poem alludes to the fact that this bear was produced to pay homage to Jerry Garcia, the American rock musician whose band–The Grateful Dead–entertained fans in the 70s, 80s, and months before his death in 1995. Garcia's birthday, August 1, 1995 combines the month and day Jerry Garcia was born and the year he died. Jerry Garcia was born on August 1, 1942, and died on August 9, 1995. Garcia was "officially" retired on May 11, 1997, and Peace, the tie-dyed bear with the peace sign on his chest was introduced.

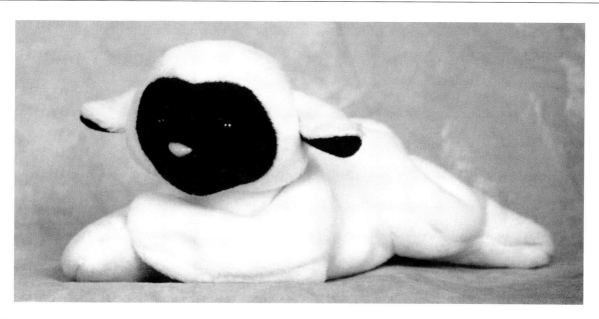

Chops, the lamb, was introduced in 1996. Chops is a cream-colored lamb with a black face and two-tone ears. He has black eyes, a triangular pink nose and a pink mouth. Chops, whose poem is derived from the Children's poem, "Mary had a Little Lamb," alludes to the fact that if you put him in the palm of your hand, he will follow you wherever you go. Rumor has it that Chops was retired because his name closely resembled Shari Lewis' popular puppet called "Lamb Chop." Chops, the lamb, was "officially" retired on January 1, 1997, when Fleece, the lamb, was chosen to take his place.

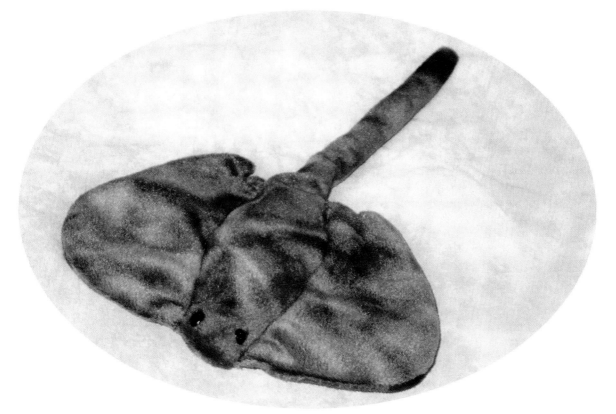

Sting, the ray, was introduced in mid-1995. He is a bluish tie-dyed ray with shades of green. His black eyes peer up from the top of his head. His body cavity and long tail are filled with pellets and stuffing. His large flat wings help him glide through the water. Sting was "officially" retired on January 1, 1997.

DATE INTRODUCED / DATE RETIRED

In order to come up with a consistent way of identifying when Beanie Babies were **INTRODUCED**, and when they were **RETIRED**, the following guidelines were set up.

Date Introduced -- This is the date that a particular Beanie Baby first appeared in a Ty catalog or New Introduction sheet. (New Introduction sheets are given to retailers mid-year for ordering newly released Beanie Babies.) We realize that Beanie Babies were in production prior to these dates, but we do not have access to that information.

Date Retired -- Prior to January 1, 1997, Ty did not make big "official" announcements when a Beanie Baby was retired. Therefore, with the exception of the Beanie Babies retired after January 1, 1997, the date given for retirement is the last catalog or New Introduction sheet that Beanie Baby appeared in.

There are certain Beanie Babies that are not pictured in any catalog or New Introduction sheet. We have determined the Date Introduced and Date Retired by the heart tag and tush tag that appear on the Beanie Baby.

Exact dates are not known when production of a certain Beanie Baby was stopped at the factories in China and Korea. If we based a Beanie Baby's retirement date on when the supply was depleted at the Ty warehouses in the United Kingdom, Canada, Germany, and the United States, this time frame would be different for each one. We do not know how large of an inventory each country had at their warehouses after production was stopped on a Beanie Baby. Because of the demand here in the United States, the supply of Beanie Babies was usually depleted before that of other locations.

Note: We do not have the dates when a certain Beanie Baby could no longer be ordered by other countries. Some Beanie Babies were "unofficially retired" in other countries before they were in the United States. We also know that certain Beanie Babies, such as Libearty, Righty and Lefty, were never shipped to other countries, therefore they were only "officially" retired in the United States.

INFORMATION GUIDE - ALL BEANIE BABIES

Information Guide

Style No	Beanie Name	Date Introduced	Date Retired	Ty Web Site Birthday	Catalog 94	95	96	97
4032	Ally, the alligator	1994*		03-14-94		●	●	●
4074	Baldy, the eagle	05-11-97*		02-17-96				●
4109	Bernie, the St. Bernard	01-01-97		10-03-96				●
4009	Bessie, the brown and white cow	1995*		06-27-95			●	●
4011	Blackie, the black bear	1994*		07-15-94		●	●	●
4163	Blizzard, the black and white tiger	05-11-97*		12-12-96				●
4001	Bones, the brown dog	1994*		01-18-94		●	●	●
4067	Bongo, the monkey with brown tail - r/w tush tag/no name	1996	1996					
4067	Bongo, the monkey with brown tail - r/w tush tag/with name	1997		08-17-95				
4067	Bongo, the monkey with tan tail - b/w tush tag	1995	1996				●	●
4067	Bongo, the monkey with tan tail - r/w tush tag/no name	1996	1996					
4067	Bongo, the monkey with tan tail - r/w tush tag/with name	1996		08-17-95				
4085	Bronty, the brontosaurus	1995*	1996				●	
4010	Brownie, the brown bear	1993	1993					
4078	Bubbles, the black and yellow fish	1995*	05-11-97	07-02-95			●	●
4016	Bucky, the beaver	1996		06-08-95			●	●
4045	Bumble, the bee	1996	1996	10-16-95			●	
4071	Caw, the crow	1995*	1996				●	
4012	Chilly, the white polar bear	1994*	1995			●		
4121	Chip, the calico cat	05-11-97*		01-26-96				●
4015	**Chocolate, the moose**	1994		04-27-93	●	●	●	●
4019	Chops, the lamb	1996	01-01-97	05-03-96			●	
4083	Claude, the tie-dyed crab	05-11-97*		09-03-96				●
4160	Congo, the gorilla	1996*		11-09-96				●
4079	Coral, the tie-dyed fish	1996	01-01-97	03-02-95			●	
4130	Crunch, the shark	01-01-97		01-13-96				●
4010	**Cubbie, the brown bear**	1994		11-14-93	●	●	●	●
4052	Curly, the brown-napped bear	1996*		04-12-96				●
4006	Daisy, the black and white cow	1994*		05-10-94		●	●	●
4008	Derby, the coarse-mane horse	1996		09-16-95			●	●
4008	Derby, the fine-mane horse	1995*	1995					
4027	Digger, the orange crab	1994*	1995			●		
4027	Digger, the red crab	1995*	05-11-97	08-23-95			●	●
4110	Doby, the doberman	01-01-97		11-09-96				●
4171	Doodle, the rooster	05-11-97*		03-08-96				●
4100	Dotty, the dalmatian	05-11-97*		10-17-96				●
4018	Ears, the brown rabbit	1996		04-18-95			●	●
4180	Echo, the dolphin	05-11-97*		12-21-96				●
4021	**Flash, the dolphin**	1994	05-11-97	05-13-93	●	●	●	●
4125	Fleece, the napped lamb	01-01-97		03-21-96				●
4012	Flip, the white cat	1996		02-28-95			●	●
4118	Floppity, the lavender bunny	01-01-97		05-28-96				●

INFORMATION GUIDE – ALL BEANIE BABIES

Style No	Beanie Name	Date Introduced	Date Retired	Ty Web Site Birthday	Catalog 94	95	96	97
4043	Flutter, the tie-dyed butterfly	1995*	1996				●	
4066	Freckles, the leopard	1996*		06-03-96				●
4051	Garcia, the tie-dyed bear	1996	05-11-97	08-01-95			●	●
4023	Goldie, the goldfish	1994*		11-14-94	●	●	●	●
4126	Gracie, the swan	01-01-97		06-17-96				●
4092	Grunt, the razorback hog	1996	05-11-97	07-19-95			●	●
4061	Happy, the gray hippo	1994*	1995			●		
4061	Happy, the lavender hippo	1995*		02-25-94			●	●
4119	Hippity, the mint green bunny	01-01-97		06-01-96				●
4073	Hoot, the owl	1996		08-09-95			●	●
4117	Hoppity, the rose bunny	01-01-97		04-03-96				●
4060	Humphrey, the camel	1994*	1995			●		
4044	Inch, the inchworm with felt antennae	1996	1996				●	●
4044	Inch, the inchworm with yarn antennae	1996		09-03-95				
4028	Inky, the pink octopus	1995*		11-29-94			●	●
4028	Inky, the tan octopus with a mouth	1995	1995					
4028	Inky, the tan octopus without a mouth	1994*	1994			●		
4082	Jolly, the walrus	05-11-97*		12-02-96				●
4070	Kiwi, the toucan	1995*	01-01-97	09-16-95			●	
4085	Lefty, the donkey with American flag	1996*	01-01-97	07-04-96				
4020	**Legs, the frog**	1994		04-25-93	●	●	●	●
4057	Libearty, the white bear with American flag	1996	01-01-97	Summer 1996				
4057	Libearty/Beani**ne**, white bear with American flag	1996*	01-01-97	Summer 1996				
4033	Lizzy, the blue lizard with black spots	1996		05-11-95			●	●
4033	Lizzy, the tie-dyed lizard	1995*	1995					
4040	Lucky, the ladybug with 7 felt dots	1994*	1996			●	●	●
4040	Lucky, the ladybug with approx. 11 dots	1996		05-01-95				
4040	Lucky, the ladybug with approx. 21 dots	1996		05-01-95				
4088	Magic, the white dragon-hot pink stitching	1996		09-05-95				
4088	Magic, the white dragon-light pink stitching	1995*		09-05-95			●	●
4081	Manny, the manatee	1996	05-11-97	06-08-95			●	●
4600	Maple/Maple, the white bear with Canadian flag	1997		07-01-96				
4600	Maple/Pride, the white bear with Canadian flag	02/97	02/97	07-01-96				
4162	Mel, the koala	01-01-97		01-15-96				●
4007	Mystic, the coarse-mane unicorn	1996		05-21-94				
4007	Mystic, the fine-mane unicorn	1994*	1995			●	●	●
4067	Nana, the monkey with tan tail - b/w tush tag	1995	1995					
4104	Nanook, the husky	05-11-97*		11-21-96				●
4003	Nip, the all gold cat with pink ears (no white)	1995	1995					
4003	Nip, the gold cat with white face and belly	1995	1995			●		
4003	Nip, the gold cat with white paws	1996		03-06-94			●	●
4114	Nuts, the squirrel	01-01-97		01-21-96				●
4025	Patti, the deep fuchsia platypus	1993	1993					
4025	Patti, the fuchsia platypus	1996		01-06-93				
4025	Patti, the magenta platypus	1995	1995					
4025	**Patti, the raspberry platypus**	1994	1994		●	●	●	●
4053	Peace, the tie-dyed bear	05-11-97*		02-01-96				

Style No	Beanie Name	Date Introduced	Date Retired	Ty Web Site Birthday	Catalog 94	95	96	97
4062	Peanut, the light blue elephant	1996		01-25-95			●	●
4062	Peanut, the royal blue elephant	1995*	1995					
4013	Peking, the panda bear	1994*	1995			●		
4026	**Pinchers, the red lobster**	1994		06-19-93		●	●	●
4072	Pinky, the pink flamingo	1996		02-13-95			●	●
4161	Pouch, the kangaroo	01-01-97		11-06-96				●
4106	Pugsly, the pug	05-11-97*		05-02-96				●
4026	Punchers, the red lobster	1993	1993		●			
4024	Quacker, the duck with wings	1995	1995					
4024	Quacker, the duck without wings	1994	1995					
4024	Quacke**rs**, the duck with wings	1995		04-19-94		●	●	●
4024	Quacke**rs**, the duck without wings	1994*	1995					
4091	Radar, the bat	1996	05-11-97	10-30-95			●	●
4086	Rex, the tyrannosaurus	1995*	1996				●	
4086	Righty, the elephant with American flag	1996*	01-01-97	07-04-96				●
4014	Ringo, the raccoon	1996		07-14-95			●	●
4069	Roary, the lion	05-11-97*		02-20-96				●
4101	Rover, the red dog	1996*		05-30-96				●
4107	Scoop, the pelican	1996*		07-01-96				●
4102	Scottie, the Scottish terrier	1996*		06-15-96				●
4029	Seamore, the seal	1994*		12-14-96		●	●	●
4080	Seaweed, the otter	1996		03-19-96			●	●
4031	Slither, the snake	1994*	1995			●		
4115	Sly, the brown-belly fox	1996*	1996	09-12-96				●
4115	Sly, the white-belly fox	1996		09-12-96				
4120	Snip, the Siamese cat	01-01-97		10-22-96				●
4002	Snort, the red bull with cream paws	01-01-97		05-15-95				●
4100	Sparky, the dalmatian	1996*	05-11-97	02-27-96				●
4030	Speedy, the turtle	1994*		08-14-94		●	●	●
4060	Spike, the rhinoceros	1996*		08-13-96				●
4022	**Splash, the orca whale**	1994	05-11-97	07-08-93	●	●	●	●
4090	Spook, the ghost	1995	1995					
4090	Spooky, the ghost	1996		10-31-95			●	●
4000	Spot, the black and white dog with a spot	1994		01-03-93		●	●	●
4000	**Spot, the black and white dog without a spot**	1994	1994		●			
4005	**Squealer, the pig**	1994		04-23-93	●	●	●	●
4087	Steg, the stegosaurus	1995*	1996				●	
4077	Sting, the ray	1995*	01-01-97	08-27-95			●	
4017	Stinky, the skunk	1995*		02-13-95			●	●
4065	Stripes, the black and orange tiger	1995*	1996				●	●
4065	Stripes, the black and tan tiger	1996		06-11-95				
4002	Tabasco, the red bull	1995*	01-01-97	05-15-95			●	
4031	Tank, the 7-line armadillo	1996	1996				●	●
4031	Tank, the 9-line armadillo	1996	1996	02-22-95				
4031	Tank, the 7-line armadillo with shell	1997		02-22-95				
4031	Tank, the 9-line armadillo with shell	1996		02-22-95				

Style No	Beanie Name	Date Introduced	Date Retired	Ty Web Site Birthday	Catalog			
					94	95	96	97
4050	Teddy, the new face-brown bear	1995		11-28-95		●	●	●
4052	Teddy, the new face-cranberry bear	1995	1995			●		
4057	Teddy, the new face-jade bear	1995	1995			●		
4056	Teddy, the new face-magenta bear	1995	1995			●		
4051	Teddy, the new face-teal bear	1995	1995			●		
4055	Teddy, the new face-violet bear	1995	1995			●		
4050	Teddy, the old face-brown bear	1994*	1995					
4052	Teddy, the old face-cranberry bear	1994*	1995					
4057	Teddy, the old face-jade bear	1994*	1995					
4056	Teddy, the old face-magenta bear	1994*	1995					
4051	Teddy, the old face-teal bear	1994*	1995					
4055	Teddy, the old face-violet bear	1994*	1995					
4042	Trap, the mouse	1994*	1995			●		
4076	Tuck, the walrus	1996	01-01-97	09-18-95				
4108	Tuffy, the terrier	05-11-97*		10-12-96				●
4076	Tusk, the walrus	1996	01-01-97	09-18-95			●	
4068	Twigs, the giraffe	1996		05-19-95			●	●
4058	Valentino, the white bear with red heart	1995		02-14-94		●	●	●
4064	Velvet, the panther	1995*		12-16-95			●	●
4075	Waddle, the penguin	1995*		12-19-95			●	●
4084	Waves, the orca whale	05-11-97*		12-08-96				●
4041	Web, the spider	1994*	1995			●		
4013	Weenie, the dachshund	1996		07-20-95			●	●
4103	Wrinkles, the bulldog	1996*		05-01-96				●
4063	Ziggy, the zebra	1995*		12-24-95			●	●
4004	Zip, the all black cat with pink ears (no white)	1995	1995					
4004	Zip, the black cat with white face and belly	1995	1995			●		
4004	Zip, the black cat with white paws	1996		03-28-94			●	●

*** Mid-year "New Introductions"**

The "Original Nine" Beanie Babies introduced in 1994 are in blue print.

The 1994 catalog lists Pinchers as the red lobster, but actually it is Punchers, the red lobster who is shown.

When Inky was first produced, he did not have a mouth. The 1994 "New Introductions" sheet,* does picture Inky with a mouth, but actually it was drawn on at a later time. This is why most of the Inkys without the mouth, have the first and second version heart tags. During the early part of 1995, Inky's mouth was sewn on, which explains why most of the Inkys with a mouth, have the third version heart tag.

The 1997 mid-year "New Introductions" include pictures of the Beanie Babies that were introduced and *retired* on May 11, 1997.

* See page 116.

Birthdays are only listed on the Beanie Babies that were still in existence when the fourth version heart tag (Ty heart tag with the yellow star that says "BEANIE ORIGINAL BABY") came out around July, 1996. Old tag Beanie Babies, without the yellow star, do not have birthdays listed on them.

Beanie Babies with the same style number

Style No	Beanie Name
4002	Tabasco and Snort
4010	Brownie and Cubbie
4012	Chilly and Flip
4013	Peking and Weenie
4026	Punchers and Pinchers
4031	Slither and Tank
4051	Teddy (old/new face) teal and Garcia
4052	Teddy (old/new face) cranberry and Curly
4057	Teddy (old/new face) jade and Libearty
4060	Humphrey and Spike
4067	Nana and Bongo
4085	Bronty and Lefty
4086	Rex and Righty
4090	Spook and Spooky
4100	Sparky and Dotty

Beanie Babies with different printed birthdates

Ty Web Site Birthdates	Other Birthdates Found	Beanie Name
06-03-96	07-28-96	Freckles, the leopard
06-15-96	06-03-96	Scottie, the Scottish terrier

Freckles™ style 4066
DATE OF BIRTH : 6 - 3 - 96

From the trees he hunts prey
In the night and in the day
He's the king of camouflage
Look real close he's no mirage!

Visit our web page!!!
http://www.ty.com

Freckles™ style 4066
DATE OF BIRTH : 7 - 28 - 96

From the trees he hunts prey
In the night and in the day
He's the king of camouflage
Look real close, he's no mirage!

Visit our web page!!!
http://www.ty.com

Scottie™ style 4102
DATE OF BIRTH : 6 - 15 - 96

Scottie is a friendly sort
Even though his legs are short
He is always happy as can be
His best friends are you and me!

Visit our web page!!!
http://www.ty.com

Scottie™ style 4102
DATE OF BIRTH : 6 - 3 - 96

Scottie is a friendly sort
Even though his legs are short
He is always happy as can be
His best friends are you and me!

Visit our web page!!!
http://www.ty.com

Style No	Beanie Name	Date Introduced	Date Retired	Ty Web Site Birthday	Catalog 94	95	96	97
4067	Bongo, the monkey with brown tail - r/w tush tag / no name	1996	1996					
4067	Bongo, the monkey with tan tail - b/w tush tag	1995	1996				●	●
4067	Bongo, the monkey with tan tail - r/w tush tag no name	1996	1996					
4085	Bronty, the brontosaurus	1995*	1996				●	
4010	Brownie, the brown bear	1993	1993					
4078	Bubbles, the black and yellow fish	1995*	05-11-97	07-02-95			●	●
4045	Bumble, the bee	1996	1996	10-16-95			●	
4071	Caw, the crow	1995*	1996				●	
4012	Chilly, the white polar bear	1994*	1995			●		
4019	Chops, the lamb	1996	01-01-97	05-03-96			●	
4079	Coral, the tie-dyed fish	1996	01-01-97	03-02-95			●	
4008	Derby, the fine-mane horse	1995*	1995					
4027	Digger, the orange crab	1994*	1995			●		
4027	Digger, the red crab	1995*	05-11-97	08-23-95			●	●
4021	Flash, the dolphin	1994	05-11-97	05-13-93	●	●	●	●
4043	Flutter, the tie-dyed butterfly	1995*	1996				●	
4051	Garcia, the tie-dyed bear	1996	05-11-97	08-01-95			●	●
4092	Grunt, the razorback hog	1996	05-11-97	07-19-95			●	●
4061	Happy, the gray hippo	1994*	1995			●		
4060	Humphrey, the camel	1994*	1995			●		
4044	Inch, the inchworm with felt antennae	1996	1996				●	●
4028	Inky, the tan octopus with a mouth	1995	1995					
4028	Inky, the tan octopus without a mouth	1994*	1994			●		
4070	Kiwi, the toucan	1995*	01-01-97	09-16-95		●		
4085	Lefty, the donkey with American flag	1996*	01-01-97	07-04-96				
4057	Libearty, the white bear with American flag	1996	01-01-97	Summer 1996				
4057	Libearty/Beanine, white bear with American flag	1996*	01-01-97	Summer 1996				
4033	Lizzy, the tie-dyed lizard	1995*	1995					
4040	Lucky, the ladybug with 7 felt dots	1994*	1996			●	●	●
4081	Manny, the manatee	1996	05-11-97	06-08-95			●	●
4600	Maple/Pride, the white bear with Canadian flag	02/97	02/97	07-01-96				
4007	Mystic, the fine-mane unicorn	1994*	1995			●	●	
4067	Nana, the monkey with tan tail - b/w tush tag	1995	1995					
4003	Nip, the all gold cat with pink ears (no white)	1995	1995					
4003	Nip, the gold cat with white face and belly	1995	1995			●		
4025	Patti, the deep fuchsia platypus	1993	1993					
4025	Patti, the magenta platypus	1995	1995					
4025	Patti, the raspberry platypus	1994	1994		●	●	●	●
4062	Peanut, the royal blue elephant	1995*	1995					
4013	Peking, the panda bear	1994*	1995			●		
4026	Punchers, the red lobster	1993	1993		●			

Style No	Beanie Name	Date Introduced	Date Retired	Ty Web Site Birthday	Catalog			
					94	95	96	97
4024	Quacker, the duck with wings	1995	1995					
4024	Quacker, the duck without wings	1994	1995					
4024	Quackers, the duck without wings	1994*	1995					
4091	Radar, the bat	1996	05-11-97	10-30-95			●	●
4086	Rex, the tyrannosaurus	1995*	1996				●	
4086	Righty, the elephant with American flag	1996*	01-01-97	07-04-96				
4031	Slither the snake	1994*	1995			●		
4115	Sly, the brown-belly fox	1996*	1996	09-12-96				●
4100	Sparky, the dalmatian	1996*	05-11-97	02-27-96				●
4022	Splash, the orca whale	1994	05-11-97	07-08-93	●	●	●	●
4090	Spook, the ghost	1995	1995					
4000	Spot, the black and white dog without a spot	1994	1994		●			
4087	Steg, the stegosaurus	1995*	1996				●	
4077	Sting, the ray	1995*	01-01-97	08-27-95			●	
4065	Stripes, the black and orange tiger	1995*	1996				●	●
4002	Tabasco, the red bull	1995*	01-01-97	05-15-95			●	
4031	Tank, the 7-line armadillo	1996	1996				●	●
4031	Tank, the 9-line armadillo	1996	1996	02-22-95				
4052	Teddy, the new face-cranberry bear	1995	1995			●		
4057	Teddy, the new face-jade bear	1995	1995			●		
4056	Teddy, the new face-magenta bear	1995	1995			●		
4051	Teddy, the new face-teal bear	1995	1995			●		
4055	Teddy, the new face-violet bear	1995	1995			●		
4050	Teddy, the old face-brown bear	1994*	1995					
4052	Teddy, the old face-cranberry bear	1994*	1995					
4057	Teddy, the old face-jade bear	1994*	1995					
4056	Teddy, the old face-magenta bear	1994*	1995					
4051	Teddy, the old face-teal bear	1994*	1995					
4055	Teddy, the old face-violet bear	1994*	1995					
4042	Trap, the mouse	1994*	1995			●		
4076	Tuck, the walrus	1996	01-01-97	09-18-95				
4076	Tusk, the walrus	1996	01-01-97	09-18-95			●	
4041	Web, the spider	1994*	1995			●		
4004	Zip, the all black cat with pink ears (no white)	1995	1995					
4004	Zip, the black cat with white face and belly	1995	1995			●		

Style No	Beanie Name
4000	Spot, the black and white dog with a spot
4000	Spot, the black and white dog without spot
4001	Bones, the brown dog
4002	Snort, the red bull with cream paws
4002	Tabasco, the red bull
4003	Nip, the all gold cat with pink ears (no white)
4003	Nip, the gold cat with white face and belly
4003	Nip, the gold cat with white paws
4004	Zip, the all black cat with pink ears (no white)
4004	Zip, the black cat with white face and belly
4004	Zip, the black cat with white paws
4005	Squealer, the pig
4006	Daisy, the black and white cow
4007	Mystic, the coarse-mane unicorn
4007	Mystic, the fine-mane unicorn
4008	Derby, the coarse-mane horse
4008	Derby, the fine-mane horse
4009	Bessie, the brown and white cow
4010	Brownie, the brown bear
4010	Cubbie, the brown bear
4011	Blackie, the black bear
4012	Chilly, the white polar bear
4012	Flip, the white cat
4013	Peking, the panda bear
4013	Weenie, the dachshund
4014	Ringo, the raccoon
4015	Chocolate, the moose
4016	Bucky, the beaver
4017	Stinky, the skunk
4018	Ears, the brown rabbit
4019	Chops, the lamb
4020	Legs, the frog
4021	Flash, the dolphin
4022	Splash, the orca whale
4023	Goldie, the goldfish
4024	Quacker, the duck with wings
4024	Quacker, the duck without wings
4024	Quacker**s**, the duck with wings
4024	Quacker**s**, the duck without wings
4025	Patti, the deep fuchsia platypus
4025	Patti, the fuchsia platypus
4025	Patti, the magenta platypus
4025	Patti, the raspberry platypus
4026	Pinchers, the red lobster
4026	Punchers, the red lobster
4027	Digger, the orange crab
4027	Digger, the red crab
4028	Inky, the pink octopus
4028	Inky, the tan octopus with a mouth
4028	Inky, the tan octopus without a mouth
4029	Seamore, the seal
4030	Speedy, the turtle
4031	Slither, the snake
4031	Tank, the 7-line armadillo

Style No	Beanie Name
4031	Tank, the 9-line armadillo
4031	Tank, the 7-line armadillo with shell
4031	Tank, the 9-line armadillo with shell
4032	Ally, the alligator
4033	Lizzy, the blue lizard with black spots
4033	Lizzy, the tie-dyed lizard
4040	Lucky, the ladybug with 7 felt dots
4040	Lucky, the ladybug with approx. 11 dots
4040	Lucky, the ladybug with approx. 21 dots
4041	Web, the spider
4042	Trap, the mouse
4043	Flutter, the tie-dyed butterfly
4044	Inch, the inchworm with felt antennae
4044	Inch, the inchworm with yarn antennae
4045	Bumble, the bee
4050	Teddy, the new face-brown bear
4050	Teddy, the old face-brown bear
4051	Garcia, the tie-dyed bear
4051	Teddy, the new face-teal bear
4051	Teddy, the old face-teal bear
4052	Curly, the brown napped bear
4052	Teddy, the new face-cranberry bear
4052	Teddy, the old face-cranberry bear
4053	Peace, the tie-dyed bear
4055	Teddy, the new face-violet bear
4055	Teddy, the old face-violet bear
4056	Teddy, the new face-magenta bear
4056	Teddy, the old face-magenta bear
4057	Libearty, the white bear with American flag
4057	Libearty/Beanine, the white bear with American flag
4057	Teddy, the new face-jade bear
4057	Teddy, the old face-jade bear
4058	Valentino, the white bear with red heart
4060	Humphrey, the camel
4060	Spike, the rhinoceros
4061	Happy, the gray hippo
4061	Happy, the lavender hippo
4062	Peanut, the light blue elephant
4062	Peanut, the royal blue elephant
4063	Ziggy, the zebra
4064	Velvet, the panther
4065	Stripes, the black and orange tiger
4065	Stripes, the black and tan tiger
4066	Freckles, the leopard
4067	Bongo, the monkey with brown tail - r/w tush tag / no name
4067	Bongo, the monkey with brown tail - r/w tush tag / with name
4067	Bongo, the monkey with tan tail - b/w tush tag
4067	Bongo, the monkey with tan tail - r/w tush tag / no name
4067	Bongo, the monkey with tan tail - r/w tush tag / with name
4067	Nana, the monkey with tan tail - b/w tush tag
4068	Twigs, the giraffe
4069	Roary, the lion
4070	Kiwi, the toucan
4071	Caw, the crow

Style No	Beanie Name
4072	Pinky, the pink flamingo
4073	Hoot, the owl
4074	Baldy, the eagle
4075	Waddle, the penguin
4076	Tuck, the walrus
4076	Tusk, the walrus
4077	Sting, the ray
4078	Bubbles, the black and yellow fish
4079	Coral, the tie-dyed fish
4080	Seaweed, the otter
4081	Manny, the manatee
4082	Jolly, the walrus
4083	Claude, the tie-dyed crab
4084	Waves, the orca whale
4085	Bronty, the brontosaurus
4085	Lefty, the donkey with American flag
4086	Rex, the tyrannosaurus
4086	Righty, the elephant with American flag
4087	Steg, the stegosaurus
4088	Magic, the white dragon-hot pink stitching
4088	Magic, the white dragon-light pink stitching
4090	Spook, the ghost
4090	Spooky, the ghost
4091	Radar, the bat
4092	Grunt, the razorback hog
4100	Dotty, the dalmatian
4100	Sparky, the dalmatian
4101	Rover, the red dog
4102	Scottie, the Scottish terrier
4103	Wrinkles, the bulldog
4104	Nanook, the husky
4106	Pugsly, the pug
4107	Scoop, the pelican
4108	Tuffy, the terrier
4109	Bernie, the St. Bernard
4110	Doby, the doberman
4114	Nuts, the squirrel
4115	Sly, the brown-belly fox
4115	Sly, the white-belly fox
4117	Hoppity, the rose bunny
4118	Floppity, the lavender bunny
4119	Hippity, the mint green bunny
4120	Snip, the Siamese cat
4121	Chip, the calico cat
4125	Fleece, the napped lamb
4126	Gracie, the swan
4130	Crunch, the shark
4160	Congo, the gorilla
4161	Pouch, the kangaroo
4162	Mel, the koala
4163	Blizzard, the black and white tiger
4171	Doodle, the rooster
4180	Echo, the dolphin
4600	Maple/Maple, the white bear with Canadian flag
4600	Maple/Pride, the white bear with Canadian flag

INFORMATION GUIDE - STYLE NUMBERS

When Ty, Inc. first introduced their plush line, attached to the Ty plush were hard **plastic** heart tags with a small "Ty" printed on them. Because of child safety regulations, these tags were removed and eventually replaced with the first version paper heart tag (swing tag).

There are **FOUR** versions of the Ty heart tag that are attached to Beanie Babies. The "Retired" Heart Tags (old tags) are the first, second, and third versions.

The first version is a single heart tag with a skinny "Ty" printed on it. It does not open like a book. The style number, name and Ty information is printed on the back of these tags. The first version heart tag appears on the "Original Nine" Beanie Babies that were produced in 1993.

The second version heart tag has the same skinny "Ty" printed on it as the first version, but now the tag opens like a book. It is also referred to as a double tag.

The third version heart tag still opens like a book, but the "Ty" has a different look. The "Ty" is now larger and more rounded. It is also referred to as a bubble Ty.

The fourth version heart tag is the same size and shape as the third version heart tag, but a yellow star that says "BEANIE ORIGINAL BABY" was added.

First version heart tag

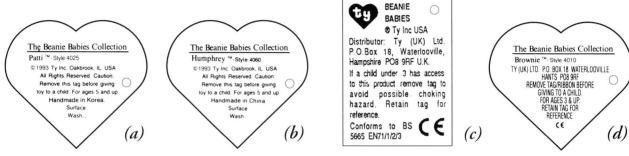

(a) (b) (c) (d)

NOTE: This was the first version Ty (UK) hang tag that was attached to Beanie Babies (c). The identifying marking "CE" was added. The Brownie tag (d) indicates that the age requirement for a child given this toy changed from "ages 5 and up" to "ages 3 and up."

Second version heart tag

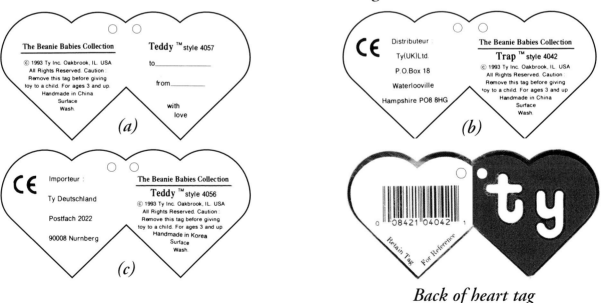

(a) (b)

(c)

Back of heart tag

Note: Example (c) has the words "Handmade in China" covered up with "Handmade in Korea." See page 93 – Heart tag cover-ups.

Third version heart tag

The Beanie Babies Collection

All Rights Reserved. Caution : Remove this tag before giving toy to a child.

Handmade in China
Surface
Wash.

Peking ™ style 4013
© Ty Inc. Oakbrook, IL. USA

to_____

from_____

with
love

(a)

The Beanie Babies Collection

© 1993 Ty Inc. Oakbrook, IL. USA
All Rights Reserved. Caution :
Remove this tag before giving
toy to a child. For ages 3 and up.
Handmade in China
Surface
Wash.

Trap ™ style 4042

to_____

from_____

with
love

(b)

Importeur Ty Deutschland
Postfach 2022 90008 Nürnberg

CE
0 08421 04013 1
Please remove all
tags and accessories
before giving this
item to a
child

Back of tag (a)

0 08421 04042 1
Retain Tag For Reference

Back of tag (b)

The Beanie Babies ™ Collection

© Ty Inc.
Oakbrook IL. U.S.A.

© Ty UK Ltd.
Waterlooville, Hants
PO8 8HH

Ty Deutschland
90008 Nürnberg

Handmade in Korea

Bumble ™ style 4045

to _____

from _____

with

love

(c)

The Beanie Babies ™ Collection

© Ty Inc.
Oakbrook IL. U.S.A.

© Ty UK Ltd.
Waterlooville, Hants
PO8 8HH

© Ty Deutschland
90008 Nürnberg

Handmade in China

Tusk ™ style 4076

to _____

from _____

with

love

(d)

Please remove all swing tags before
this item to a child under 36 months.

CE
0 08421 04045 2
Retain Tag For Reference
Surface
Wash

Back of tag (c)

Please remove all swing tags
before giving this item to a child

CE
0 08421 04076 6
Retain Tag For Reference
Surface
Wash

Back of tag (d)

NOTE: This rare tag (a) has been found on several Beanie Babies including: Peking, Chilly, Trap, and Web. When all three Ty locations were listed (c and d) on this third version heart tag, the child safety regulations were transferred to the back.

Fourth version heart tag

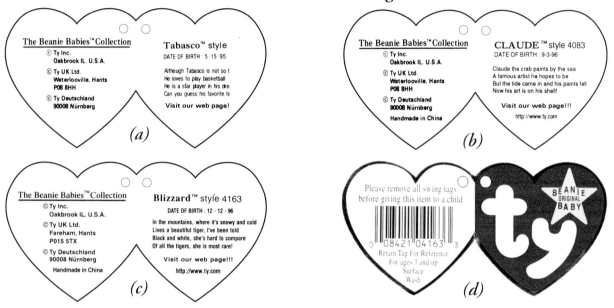

The Beanie Babies™ Collection

ⓒ Ty Inc.
Oakbrook IL. U.S.A.

ⓒ Ty UK Ltd.
Waterlooville, Hants
PO8 8HH

ⓒ Ty Deutschland
90008 Nürnberg

Tabasco™ style

DATE OF BIRTH : 5·15·95

Although Tabasco is not so t
He loves to play basketball
He is a star player in his dre
Can you guess his favorite te

Visit our web page!

(a)

The Beanie Babies™ Collection

ⓒ Ty Inc.
Oakbrook IL. U.S.A.

ⓒ Ty UK Ltd.
Waterlooville, Hants
PO8 8HH

ⓒ Ty Deutschland
90008 Nürnberg

Handmade in China

CLAUDE™ style 4083

DATE OF BIRTH : 9-3-96

Claude the crab paints by the sea
A famous artist he hopes to be
But the tide came in and his paints fell
Now his art is on his shell!

Visit our web page!!!

http://www.ty.com

(b)

The Beanie Babies™ Collection

ⓒ Ty Inc.
Oakbrook IL. U.S.A.

ⓒ Ty UK Ltd.
Fareham, Hants
PO15 5TX

ⓒ Ty Deutschland
90008 Nürnberg

Handmade in China

Blizzard™ style 4163

DATE OF BIRTH : 12 - 12 - 96

In the mountains, where it's snowy and cold
Lives a beautiful tiger, I've been told
Black and white, she's hard to compare
Of all the tigers, she is most rare!

Visit our web page!!!

http://www.ty.com

(c)

Please remove all swing tags
before giving this item to a child

0 08421 04163 3

Retain Tag For Reference
For ages 3 and up
Surface
Wash

(d)

The name of the country where the Beanie Baby was produced (Korea and China) is printed on the heart tag (a and b), as well as the tush tag.

Some of the Beanie Babies' names are printed in all capital letters (b).

The Ty UK address has changed from Waterlooville, Hants to Fareham, Hants (c).

Heart Tag Fasteners

These plastic strips attach the heart tag to the Beanie Baby. They come in two colors, red and clear. The majority of the heart tags are attached with the red strip. Both of these colors have been used to attach the heart tag to the Beanie Baby as far back as the 1994 introductions. These strips are approximately 1/2" and 3/4" in size.

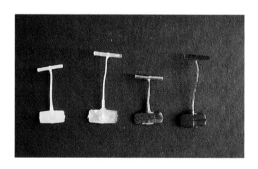

The first tush tag (body tag) was black and white and was created in 1993. In the majority of cases, the type of tush tag that your Beanie Baby has indicates the age of your Beanie Baby, but there are exceptions. There is no 1994 tush tag. The Beanie Babies produced in 1994 have the 1993 black and white tush tag. The name of the country where the Beanie Babies were produced, Korea or China, is printed on the tush tag.

The first version tush tag was black and white. It was produced in 1993 and 1995.

© 1993 TY INC., OAKBROOK IL. U.S.A. ALL RIGHTS RESERVED HAND MADE IN KOREA	ALL NEW MATERIAL POLYESTER FIBER & P.V.C. PELLETS PA. REG #1965

© 1993 TY INC., OAKBROOK IL. U.S.A. ALL RIGHTS RESERVED HAND MADE IN KOREA SURFACE WASHABLE	ALL NEW MATERIAL POLYESTER FIBER & P.V.C. PELLETS PA. REG #1965 FOR AGES 3 AND UP	© 1995 TY INC., OAKBROOK IL. U.S.A. ALL RIGHTS RESERVED HAND MADE IN KOREA SURFACE WASHABLE	ALL NEW MATERIAL POLYESTER FIBER & P.V.C. PELLETS **CE** PA. REG #1965 FOR AGES 3 AND UP
© 1993 TY INC., OAKBROOK IL. U.S.A. ALL RIGHTS RESERVED HAND MADE IN CHINA SURFACE WASHABLE	ALL NEW MATERIAL POLYESTER FIBER & P.V.C. PELLETS **CE** PA. REG #1965 FOR AGES 3 AND UP	© 1995 TY INC., OAKBROOK IL. U.S.A. ALL RIGHTS RESERVED HAND MADE IN CHINA SURFACE WASHABLE	ALL NEW MATERIAL POLYESTER FIBER & P.V.C. PELLETS PA. REG #1965 FOR AGES 3 AND UP

The identifying marking "CE" is also printed on some of these first version tush tags.
When the identifying marking "CE" was added to some of these tush tags, "FOR AGES 3 AND UP" was eliminated.

The second version tush tag was red and white. It has 1993 or 1995 printed on it. The name of the Beanie Baby does not appear on the tag.

HAND MADE IN KOREA © 1993 TY INC., OAKBROOK IL. U.S.A. SURFACE WASHABLE ALL NEW MATERIAL POLYESTER FIBER & P.V.C. PELLETS REG. NO PA-1965(KR) FOR AGES 3 AND UP **CE**

HAND MADE IN CHINA © 1993 TY INC., OAKBROOK IL. U.S.A. SURFACE WASHABLE ALL NEW MATERIAL POLYESTER FIBER & P.V.C. PELLETS REG. NO PA-1965(KR) FOR AGES 3 AND UP **CE**

HAND MADE IN KOREA © 1995 TY INC., OAKBROOK IL. U.S.A. SURFACE WASHABLE ALL NEW MATERIAL POLYESTER FIBER & P.V.C. PELLETS REG. NO PA-1965(KR) FOR AGES 3 AND UP **CE**

HAND MADE IN CHINA © 1995 TY INC., OAKBROOK IL. U.S.A. SURFACE WASHABLE ALL NEW MATERIAL POLYESTER FIBER & P.V.C. PELLETS REG. NO PA-1965(KR) FOR AGES 3 AND UP **CE**

CE: "CE" stands for "Conformite Europeene". This identifying marking indicates that the product complies with the essential requirements for health, safety, environment and consumer protection for the European market; however, it is not a guarantee of quality. This mark is required for products to enter European customs, and move freely from country to country.

On some of these later second version tush tags, "FOR AGES 3 AND UP" was eliminated.

HAND MADE IN KOREA
© 1993 TY INC.,
OAKBROOK IL. U.S.A.
SURFACE WASHABLE
ALL NEW MATERIAL
POLYESTER FIBER &
P.V.C. PELLETS
REG. NO PA-1965(KR)
CE

HAND MADE IN CHINA
© 1993 TY INC.,
OAKBROOK IL. U.S.A.
SURFACE WASHABLE
ALL NEW MATERIAL
POLYESTER FIBER &
P.V.C. PELLETS
REG. NO PA-1965(KR)
CE

HAND MADE IN KOREA
© 1995 TY INC.,
OAKBROOK IL. U.S.A.
SURFACE WASHABLE
ALL NEW MATERIAL
POLYESTER FIBER &
P.V.C. PELLETS
REG. NO PA-1965(KR)
CE

HAND MADE IN CHINA
© 1995 TY INC.,
OAKBROOK IL. U.S.A.
SURFACE WASHABLE
ALL NEW MATERIAL
POLYESTER FIBER &
P.V.C. PELLETS
REG. NO PA-1965(KR)
CE

The third version is also red and white, but now the name of the Beanie Baby appears on the tag. It has 1993, 1995 or 1996 printed on it.

The
Beanie Babies
Collection™

SPOT

HANDMADE IN KOREA
© 1993 TY INC.,
OAKBROOK IL. U.S.A
SURFACE WASHABLE
ALL NEW MATERIAL
POLYESTER FIBER
& P.V.C. PELLETS **CE**
REG. NO PA.1965 (KR)

The
Beanie Babies
Collection™

SPOT

HANDMADE IN CHINA
© 1993 TY INC.,
OAKBROOK IL. U.S.A
SURFACE WASHABLE
ALL NEW MATERIAL
POLYESTER FIBER
& P.V.C. PELLETS **CE**
REG. NO PA.1965 (KR)

The
Beanie Babies
Collection™

STRIPES

HANDMADE IN KOREA
© 1995 TY INC.,
OAKBROOK IL. U.S.A
SURFACE WASHABLE
ALL NEW MATERIAL
POLYESTER FIBER
& P.V.C. PELLETS **CE**
REG. NO PA.1965 (KR)

The
Beanie Babies
Collection™

SPOOKY

HANDMADE IN CHINA
© 1995 TY INC.,
OAKBROOK IL. U.S.A
SURFACE WASHABLE
ALL NEW MATERIAL
POLYESTER FIBER
& P.V.C. PELLETS **CE**
REG. NO PA.1965 (KR)

The
Beanie Babies
Collection™

SPARKY

HANDMADE IN KOREA
© 1996 TY INC.,
OAKBROOK IL. U.S.A
SURFACE WASHABLE
ALL NEW MATERIAL
POLYESTER FIBER
& P.V.C. PELLETS **CE**
REG. NO PA.1965 (KR)

The
Beanie Babies
Collection™

SLY

HANDMADE IN CHINA
© 1996 TY INC.,
OAKBROOK IL. U.S.A
SUFRACE WASHABLE
ALL NEW MATERIAL
POLYESTER FIBER
& P.V.C. PELLETS **CE**
REG. NO PA.1965 (KR)

Note: On the Sly tag, "Surface" is spelled "Sufrace." See page 89.

These fourth version tush tags were introduced in mid-1997. While permanent tush tags were being produced, temporary stickers with a star printed on them were used.

The
Beanie Babies
Collection™

BONES

HANDMADE IN KOREA
© 1993 TY INC.,
OAKBROOK IL. U.S.A.
SURFACE WASHABLE
ALL NEW MATERIAL
POLYESTER FIBER
& P.V.C. PELLETS **CE**
REG. NO PA.1965 (KR)

The
Beanie Babies
Collection™

BONES

HANDMADE IN CHINA
© 1993 TY INC.,
OAKBROOK IL. U.S.A
SURFACE WASHABLE
ALL NEW MATERIAL
POLYESTER FIBER
& P.V.C. PELLETS **CE**
REG. NO PA.1965 (KR)

The
Beanie Babies
Collection™

ZIGGY

HANDMADE IN KOREA
© 1995 TY INC.,
OAKBROOK IL. U.S.A
SURFACE WASHABLE
ALL NEW MATERIAL
POLYESTER FIBER
& P.V.C. PELLETS **CE**
REG. NO PA.1965 (KR)

The
Beanie Babies
Collection™

ZIGGY

HANDMADE IN CHINA
© 1995 TY INC.,
OAKBROOK IL. U.S.A
SURFACE WASHABLE
ALL NEW MATERIAL
POLYESTER FIBER
& P.V.C. PELLETS **CE**
REG. NO PA.1965 (KR)

The
Beanie Babies
Collection™

ROVER

HANDMADE IN KOREA
© 1996 TY INC.,
OAKBROOK IL. U.S.A
SURFACE WASHABLE
ALL NEW MATERIAL
POLYESTER FIBER
& P.V.C. PELLETS **CE**
REG. NO PA.1965 (KR)

The
Beanie Babies
Collection™

ROVER

HANDMADE IN CHINA
© 1996 TY INC.,
OAKBROOK IL. U.S.A
SURFACE WASHABLE
ALL NEW MATERIAL
POLYESTER FIBER
& P.V.C. PELLETS **CE**
REG. NO PA.1965 (KR)

The Canadian tush tag is a larger black and white tag. It is attached to all Beanie Babies that were produced exclusively for Canada. The information on this tag is written in English and French.

Not to be removed until delivered to the consumer	Ne pas enlever avant livraison au consommateur		Not to be removed until delivered to the consumer	Ne pas enlever avant livraison au consommateur
This label is affixed in compliance with the Upholstered and Stuffed Articles Act	Cette étiquette est apposée conformément à loi sur les articles rembourrés		This label is affixed in compliance with the Upholstered and Stuffed Articles Act	Cette étiquette est apposée conformément à loi sur les articles rembourrés
This article contains NEW MATERIAL ONLY	Cet article contient MATÉRIAU NEUF SEULEMENT		This article contains NEW MATERIAL ONLY	Cet article contient MATÉRIAU NEUF SEULEMENT
Made by Ont. Reg. No. **20B6484**	Fabriqué par No d'enrg. Ont. **20B6484**		Made by Ont. Reg. No. **20B6484**	Fabriqué par No d'enrg. Ont. **20B6484**
Contents: Plastic Pellets Polyesters Fibers Made in Korea	Contenu:Boulette de plastique Fibres de Polyester Fabriqué en Corée		Contents: Plastic Pellets Polyesters Fibers Made in China	Contenu:Boulette de plastique Fibres de Polyester Fabriqué en Chine

TY INC., © 1994
OAKBROOK IL.
REG-NO. PA-1965 (KR)
ALL NEW MATERIAL
CONTENTS: POLYESTER
HAND MADE IN CHINA
FOR ALL AGES

This embroidered cloth Ty tush tag has also been found attached to some Beanie Babies. The majority of Beanie Babies that have this tush tag, also have the 2nd version heart tag, as well as, the Canadian tush tag. The embroidered tag is primarily used for other Ty products such as the plush line. Because of human error and language differences, this tag was accidentally attached to some Beanies Babies when a changeover was being made from a plush production run to a Beanie Baby run.

EXCEPTIONS

The method that Ty, Inc. chose to date a Beanie Babies' tush tag is different for some Beanie Babies. There are certain tush tags that do not list the year when the Beanie Baby was produced, but rather the year that its predecessor was produced.

Example: Garcia the tie-dyed bear

Garcia has a 1993 tush tag even though he was produced in 1995 and should have a 1995 tush tag. Why? Garcia was given the date of his predecessor, Teddy, the old-face bear, who was produced in 1993.

These are the Beanie Babies that have the 1993 tush tag even though they were introduced in 1995/1996:

Curly, the napped bear
Digger, the red crab
Flip, the white cat
Garcia, the tie-dyed bear
Happy, the lavender hippo
Inky, the tan octopus with a mouth
Inky, the pink octopus
Lucky, the ladybug with approx. 11 dots
Lucky, the ladybug with approx. 21 dots
Mystic, the coarse-mane unicorn
Nip, the all gold cat with pink ears (no white)
Nip, the gold cat with white paws
Patti, the fuchsia platypus
Patti, the magenta platypus
Quacker, the duck with wings
Quacker**s**, the duck with wings
Teddy, the new face-brown bear
Teddy, the new face-cranberry bear
Teddy, the new face-jade bear
Teddy, the new face-magenta bear
Teddy, the new face-teal bear
Teddy, the new face-violet bear
Valentino, the white bear with red heart
Zip, the all black cat with pink ears (no white)
Zip, the black cat with white paws

Ty Tags Chronology

Style No	Beanie Name	Hang Tags 1st	2nd	3rd	4th	1993 b/w	1995 b/w	1993 red NO Name	1995 red NO Name	1993 red With Name	1995 red With Name	1996 red With Name
1993 Introductions												
4010	Brownie	X				X						
4025	Patti-deep fuchsia	X				X						
4026	Punchers	X				X						
Original Nine - 1994 Introductions												
4015	Chocolate		X	X	X	X		X		X		
4010	Cubbie		X	X	X	X		X		X		
4021	Flash		X	X	X	X		X		X		
4020	Legs		X	X	X	X		X		X		
4025	Patti-raspberry		X			X						
4026	Pinchers		X	X	X	X		X		X		
4022	Splash		X	X	X	X		X		X		
4000	Spot-without a spot		X			X						
4005	Squealer		X	X	X	X		X		X		
1994 Mid-Year New Introductions												
4032	Ally	X	X	X	X	X		X		X		
4011	Blackie	X	X	X	X	X		X		X		
4001	Bones	X	X	X	X	X		X		X		
4012	Chilly	X	X	X		X						
4006	Daisy	X	X	X	X	X		X		X		
4027	Digger-orange	X	X	X		X						
4023	Goldie	X	X	X	X	X		X		X		
4061	Happy-gray	X	X	X		X						
4060	Humphrey	X	X	X		X						
4028	Inky-tan without a mouth	X	X			X						
4040	Lucky-7 dots	X	X	X		X		X				
4007	Mystic-fine-mane	X	X	X		X		X				
4013	Peking	X	X	X		X						
4024	Quackers-without wings	X				X						
4029	Seamore	X	X	X	X	X		X		X		
4031	Slither	X	X	X		X						
4030	Speedy	X	X	X	X	X		X		X		
4050	Teddy-OF brown	X	X			X						
4052	Teddy-OF cranberry	X	X			X						
4057	Teddy-OF jade	X	X			X						
4056	Teddy-OF magenta	X	X			X						
4051	Teddy-OF teal	X	X			X						
4055	Teddy-OF violet	X	X			X						

TY TAGS CHRONOLOGY

Style No	Beanie Name	1st	2nd	3rd	4th	1993 b/w	1995 b/w	1993 red NO Name	1995 red NO Name	1993 red With Name	1995 red With Name	1996 red With Name
		Hang Tags										
4042	Trap	X	X	X								
4041	Web	X	X	X								
Other 1994 Introductions												
4024	Quacker-without wings		X			X						
4000	Spot-with spot		X	X	X	X		X		X		
1995 Introductions												
4003	Nip-gold/white-belly		X	X		X						
4024	Quacker-with wings		X			X						
4050	Teddy-NF brown		X	X	X	X		X		X		
4052	Teddy-NF cranberry		X	X		X						
4057	Teddy-NF jade		X	X		X						
4056	Teddy-NF magenta		X	X		X						
4051	Teddy-NF teal		X	X		X						
4055	Teddy-NF violet		X	X		X						
4058	Valentino		X	X	X	X		X		X		
4004	Zip-black/white-belly		X	X		X						
Other 1995 Introductions												
4028	Inky-tan with mouth		X	X		X						
4067	Nana-tan tail-b/w tush			X			X					
4003	Nip-all gold			X		X						
4025	Patti-magenta			X		X						
4024	Quackers-with wings			X	X	X		X		X		
4090	Spook			X	X		X		X			
4004	Zip-all black			X		X						
1995 Mid-Year New Introductions												
4009	Bessie			X	X		X		X		X	
4067	Bongo-tan tail-b/w tush tag			X			X					
4085	Bronty			X			X		X			
4078	Bubbles			X	X		X		X		X	
4071	Caw			X			X		X			
4008	Derby-fine-mane			X			X		X			
4027	Digger-red			X	X	X		X		X		
4043	Flutter			X			X		X			
4061	Happy-lavender			X	X	X		X		X		
4028	Inky-pink			X	X	X		X		X		
4070	Kiwi			X	X		X		X		X	
4033	Lizzy-tie-dyed			X			X					
4088	Magic-light pink stitching			X	X		X		X		X	

Style No	Beanie Name	Hang Tags 1st	2nd	3rd	4th	1993 b/w	1995 b/w	1993 red NO Name	1995 red NO Name	1993 red With Name	1995 red With Name	1996 red With Name
4062	Peanut-royal blue			X			X		X			
4086	Rex			X	X		X		X			
4087	Steg			X	X		X		X			
4077	Sting			X	X		X		X		X	
4017	Stinky			X	X		X		X		X	
4065	Stripes-black/orange			X			X		X			
4002	Tabasco			X	X		X		X		X	
4064	Velvet			X	X		X		X		X	
4075	Waddle			X	X		X		X		X	
4063	Ziggy			X	X		X		X		X	
1996 Introductions												
4016	Bucky			X	X				X		X	
4045	Bumble			X	X		X		X		X	
4019	Chops			X	X				X		X	
4079	Coral			X	X		X		X		X	
4008	Derby-coarse-mane			X	X		X		X		X	
4018	Ears			X	X				X		X	
4012	Flip			X	X			X		X		
4051	Garcia			X	X			X		X		
4092	Grunt			X	X				X		X	
4073	Hoot			X	X				X		X	
4044	Inch-felt antennae			X	X		X		X		X	
4033	Lizzy-blue with black spots			X	X		X		X		X	
4081	Manny			X	X				X		X	
4007	Mystic-coarse-mane			X	X		X	X		X		
4003	Nip-gold/white paws			X	X			X		X		
4025	Patti-fuchsia			X	X	X		X		X		
4062	Peanut-light blue			X	X		X		X		X	
4072	Pinky			X	X		X		X		X	
4091	Radar			X	X		X		X		X	
4014	Ringo			X	X				X		X	
4080	Seaweed			X	X				X		X	
4090	Spooky			X	X		X		X		X	
4031	Tank-7-line			X	X		X		X		X	
4076	Tusk			X	X				X		X	
4068	Twigs			X	X				X		X	
4013	Weenie			X	X				X		X	

Style No	Beanie Name	Hang Tags 1st	2nd	3rd	4th	1993 b/w	1995 b/w	1993 red NO Name	1995 red NO Name	1993 red With Name	1995 red With Name	1996 red With Name
4004	Zip-black/white paws			X	X			X		X		
1996 Mid-Year New Introductions												
4160	Congo				X							X
4052	Curly				X					X		
4066	Freckles				X							X
4085	Lefty				X							X
4057	Libearty/Beanine				X							X
4086	Righty				X						X	
4101	Rover				X							X
4107	Scoop				X							X
4102	Scottie				X							X
4115	Sly-brown-belly				X							X
4100	Sparky				X							X
4060	Spike				X							X
4103	Wrinkles				X							X
Other 1996 Introductions												
4067	Bongo-brown tail-red tush tag/no name			X					X			
4067	Bongo-tan tail-red tush tag/no name			X					X			
4067	Bongo-tan tail-red tush tag/with name				X						X	
4044	Inch-yarn antennae				X						X	
4057	Libearty				X							X
4040	Lucky-11 dots				X					X		
4040	Lucky-21 dots				X					X		
4088	Magic-hot pink stitching				X						X	
4115	Sly-white-belly				X							X
4065	Stripes-black/tan				X						X	
4031	Tank 9-line				X						X	
4031	Tank 9-line with shell				X						X	
4076	Tuck				X						X	
1997 Introductions												
4109	Bernie				X							X
4130	Crunch				X							X
4110	Doby				X							X
4125	Fleece				X							X
4118	Floppity-lavender				X							X
4126	Gracie				X							X
4119	Hippity-mint				X							X
4117	Hoppity-rose				X							X

Style No	Beanie Name	Hang Tags 1st	2nd	3rd	4th	1993 b/w	1995 b/w	1993 red NO Name	1995 red NO Name	1993 red With Name	1995 red With Name	1996 red With Name
4162	Mel				X							X
4114	Nuts				X							X
4161	Pouch				X							X
4120	Snip				X							X
4002	Snort				X						X	
Other 1997 Introductions												
4067	Bongo-brown tail-red tush tag/with name										X	
4600	Maple/Maple				X							X
4600	Maple/Pride				X							X
4031	Tank-7-line with shell				X						X	
1997 Mid-Year New Introductions												
4074	Baldy				X							X
4163	Blizzard				X							X
4121	Chip				X							X
4083	Claude				X							X
4171	Doodle				X							X
4100	Dotty				X							X
4180	Echo				X							X
4082	Jolly				X							X
4104	Nanook				X							X
4053	Peace				X							X
4106	Pugsly				X							X
4069	Roary				X							X
4108	Tuffy				X							X
4084	Waves				X							X

NOTE: The embroidered cloth Ty tush tag has also been found attached to some Beanie Babies. The majority of Beanie Babies that have this tush tag, have the 2nd version heart tag, as well as the Canadian tush tag. The embroidered tag is primarily used for other Ty products such as the plush line. Because of language differences and human error, this tag was accidentally attached to some Beanie Babies when a changeover was being made from a plush product run to a Beanie Baby run.

TY TAGS ALPHABETICAL

Style No	Beanie Name	1st	2nd	3rd	4th	1993 b/w	1995 b/w	1993 red NO Name	1995 red No Name	1993 red WITH Name	1995 red WITH Name	1996 red WITH Name
4032	Ally	X	X	X	X	X		X		X		
4074	Baldy				X							X
4109	Bernie				X							X
4009	Bessie			X	X		X		X		X	
4011	Blackie	X	X	X	X	X		X		X		
4163	Blizzard				X							X
4001	Bones	X	X	X	X	X		X		X		
4067	Bongo-brown tail-red tush tag/no name			X								
4067	Bongo-brown tail-red tush tag/with name				X				X		X	
4067	Bongo-tan tail-b/w tush tag			X			X					
4067	Bongo-tan tail-red tush tag/no name			X					X			
4067	Bongo-tan tail-red tush tag/with name				X						X	
4085	Bronty			X			X		X		X	
4010	Brownie	X				X						
4078	Bubbles		X	X	X		X		X		X	
4016	Bucky			X	X				X		X	
4045	Bumble			X	X		X		X		X	
4071	Caw			X			X		X			
4012	Chilly	X	X	X		X						
4121	Chip				X							X
4015	Chocolate	X	X	X	X	X		X		X		
4019	Chops			X	X				X		X	
4083	Claude				X							X
4160	Congo				X		X					X
4079	Coral			X	X		X		X		X	
4130	Crunch				X	X						
4010	Cubbie	X	X	X	X	X		X		X		
4052	Curly				X					X		
4006	Daisy	X	X	X	X	X		X		X		
4008	Derby-coarse-mane			X	X		X		X		X	
4008	Derby-fine-mane			X			X		X			
4027	Digger-orange	X	X	X	X	X		X				
4027	Digger-red				X	X				X		
4110	Doby				X							X
4171	Doodle				X							X
4100	Dotty				X				X			X
4018	Ears			X	X						X	
4180	Echo				X							X

Style No	Beanie Name	Hang Tags 1st	2nd	3rd	4th	1993 b/w	1995 b/w	1993 red NO Name	1995 red No Name	1993 red WITH Name	1995 red WITH Name	1996 red WITH Name
4021	Flash	X	X	X	X	X		X		X		
4125	Fleece				X							X
4012	Flip			X	X			X		X		
4118	Floppity-lavender			X	X							X
4043	Flutter			X			X		X			
4066	Freckles				X							X
4051	Garcia	X	X	X	X			X		X		
4023	Goldie	X	X	X	X	X		X		X		
4126	Gracie				X							X
4092	Grunt			X	X				X		X	
4061	Happy-gray	X	X	X		X						
4061	Happy-lavender			X	X	X		X		X		
4119	Hippity-mint				X							X
4073	Hoot			X	X				X		X	
4117	Hoppity-rose	X	X	X	X	X						X
4060	Humphrey	X	X	X	X	X						
4044	Inch-felt antennae			X	X		X		X		X	
4044	Inch-yarn antennae				X						X	
4028	Inky-pink			X	X	X		X		X		
4028	Inky-tan with mouth		X	X		X						
4028	Inky-tan without a mouth	X	X			X						
4082	Jolly				X		X					X
4070	Kiwi			X	X				X		X	X
4085	Lefty				X							
4020	Legs	X	X	X	X	X		X		X		
4057	Libearty				X							X
4057	Libearty/Beanine				X							X
4033	Lizzy-blue with black spots			X	X		X		X		X	
4033	Lizzy-tie-dyed			X			X					
4040	Lucky-7 dots	X	X	X		X		X				
4040	Lucky-11 dots				X					X		
4040	Lucky-21 dots				X					X		
4088	Magic-hot pink stitching				X						X	
4088	Magic-light pink stitching			X	X				X		X	
4081	Manny			X	X		X		X		X	
4600	Maple/Maple				X							X

Style No	Beanie Name	Hang Tags 1st	2nd	3rd	4th	1993 b/w	1995 b/w	1993 red NO Name	1995 red No Name	1993 red WITH Name	1995 red WITH Name	1996 red WITH Name
4600	Maple/Pride				X							X
4162	Mel				X							X
4007	Mystic-coarse-mane	X		X	X	X		X		X		
4007	Mystic-fine-mane		X	X		X		X				
4067	Nana-tan tail-b/w tush			X			X					
4104	Nanook				X							X
4003	Nip-all gold			X		X						
4003	Nip-gold/white belly		X	X		X						
4003	Nip-gold/white paws			X	X			X		X		
4114	Nuts				X							X
4025	Patti-deep fuchsia	X				X						
4025	Patti-fuchsia			X		X		X		X		
4025	Patti-magenta			X		X						
4025	Patti-raspberry	X	X			X						
4053	Peace				X							X
4062	Peanut-light blue			X	X		X		X		X	
4062	Peanut-royal blue			X			X					
4013	Peking	X	X	X		X						
4026	Pinchers	X	X	X	X	X		X				
4072	Pinky			X	X		X		X		X	
4161	Pouch				X							
4106	Pugsly				X							X
4026	Punchers	X				X						
4024	Quacker-with wings		X			X						
4024	Quacker-without wings		X	X	X	X						
4024	Quackers-with wings			X	X			X		X		
4024	Quackers-without wings	X				X						
4091	Radar			X	X		X		X		X	
4086	Rex			X			X		X			
4086	Righty				X						X	
4014	Ringo			X	X				X		X	
4069	Roary				X							X
4101	Rover				X							X
4107	Scoop				X							X
4102	Scottie				X							X
4029	Seamore	X	X	X	X	X		X		X		
4080	Seaweed			X	X			X			X	
4031	Slither	X	X	X		X						
4115	Sly-brown-belly				X							X

Style No	Beanie Name	Hang Tags 1st	2nd	3rd	4th	1993 b/w	1995 b/w	1993 red NO Name	1995 red No Name	1993 red WITH Name	1995 red WITH Name	1996 red WITH Name
4115	Sly-white-belly				X							X
4120	Snip				X							X
4002	Snort				X						X	
4100	Sparky				X							X
4030	Speedy	X	X	X	X	X		X		X		
4060	Spike				X							X
4022	Splash	X	X	X	X	X		X		X		
4090	Spook			X			X		X			
4090	Spooky			X	X				X		X	
4000	Spot-with spot		X	X	X	X		X		X		
4000	Spot-without a spot	X	X	X		X						
4005	Squealer	X	X	X	X	X		X		X		
4087	Steg			X			X		X			
4077	Sting			X	X		X		X		X	
4017	Stinky			X	X		X		X		X	
4065	Stripes-black/orange						X		X			
4065	Stripes-black/tan				X				X		X	
4002	Tabasco			X	X		X		X		X	
4031	Tank-7-line		X	X	X		X		X		X	
4031	Tank-9-line				X						X	
4031	Tank-7-line with shell				X						X	
4031	Tank-9-line with shell				X						X	
4050	Teddy-NF brown			X	X	X		X		X		
4052	Teddy-NF cranberry		X	X		X						
4057	Teddy-NF jade		X	X		X						
4056	Teddy-NF magenta		X	X		X						
4051	Teddy-NF teal		X	X		X						
4055	Teddy-NF violet		X	X		X						
4050	Teddy-OF brown	X	X			X						
4052	Teddy-OF cranberry	X	X			X						
4057	Teddy-OF jade	X	X			X						
4056	Teddy-OF magenta	X	X			X						
4051	Teddy-OF teal	X	X			X						
4055	Teddy-OF violet	X	X			X						
4042	Trap	X	X	X		X						
4076	Tuck				X						X	
4108	Tuffy				X							X
4076	Tusk			X	X		X		X		X	

Style No	Beanie Name	Hang Tags 1st	2nd	3rd	4th	1993 b/w	1995 b/w	1993 red NO Name	1995 red No Name	1993 red WITH Name	1995 red WITH Name	1996 red WITH Name
4068	Twigs			X	X				X		X	
4058	Valentino		X	X	X	X		X		X		
4064	Velvet			X	X		X		X		X	
4075	Waddle			X	X		X		X		X	
4084	Waves				X							X
4041	Web	X	X	X		X						
4013	Weenie			X	X				X		X	
4103	Wrinkles				X							X
4063	Ziggy			X	X		X		X		X	
4004	Zip-all black			X		X						
4004	Zip-black/white belly		X	X		X						
4004	Zip-black/white paws			X	X			X		X		

NOTE: The embroidered cloth Ty tush tag has also been found attached to some Beanie Babies. The majority of Beanie Babies that have this tush tag, have the 2nd version heart tag, as well as the Canadian tush tag. The embroidered tag is primarily used for other Ty products such as the plush line. Because of language differences and human error, this tag was accidentally attached to some Beanie Babies when a changeover was being made from a plush product run to a Beanie Baby run.

When Beanie Babies were first produced, mistakes were seldom made. However, since January 1997, as more Beanie Babies were mass-produced to accommodate the insatiable demand, more of these mistakes have appeared at an increasing rate.

Beanie Baby mistakes are classified into four categories: Mistagged Beanie Babies, Tag Misprints, Manufacturing Oddities and Tag Cover-Ups.

Because of the mass production of more than 80 different Beanie Babies in countries where English is not the primary language, it has become quite common to find Beanie Babies with either an incorrect heart tag, an incorrect tush tag, or both.

Heart Tag: (swing tag)

Although some people like to collect mistagged Beanie Babies, those that do, tend to stay away from Beanie Babies with incorrect heart tags. There are several reasons for not collecting Beanie Babies with incorrect heart tags:

1. Heart tags are easy to remove; therefore they can be switched easily. There is no way of proving that an incorrect heart tag was put on at the factory or at a later date.
2. Half the fun of getting Beanie Babies, especially for children, is to have a record of the birthday and poem of that particular Beanie Baby, not those of another.
3. Once a swing tag is removed from a mistagged Beanie, that Beanie is no longer unusual or unique.

Tush Tag: (body tag)

Prior to mid-1996, incorrect tush tags were quite uncommon. Up until then, the only mistake was the occasional appearance of the embroidered tush tag reserved for use on other Ty products. However, once tush tags came out with the Beanie Babies' name on them, all kinds of mistagged Beanie Babies have appeared on the market.

A notable tush tag mistake occurred in 1997 when Ty Canada released the Canadian bear, Maple. Maple was originally to have been named Pride, but underwent a name change before being released to the public. However, about 3,000 had already been made with the Pride name on the tush tag and they were distributed with a Maple swing tag.

Another mistake occurred in April 1997, when Sparky the dalmatian started showing up with Dotty tush tags. This mistake instantly alerted the public that a new dalmatian, although not announced or released yet, was already in production by Ty.

A large number of typographical and grammatical errors have been found on Beanie Baby swing and tush tags. We are not sure where the tags are printed, but it is most likely in China or Korea where the Beanie Babies are made. These misprints are primarily a result of tags being typed up by people whose primary language is not English. In some cases, these errors were corrected on the next production run for that tag, but sometimes new errors were made.

Heart Tags: (swing tags)

One of the more notable swing tag misprints occurred during the latter part of 1996 when Tusk the walrus came out with the misspelling of "Tuck" on its swing tag.

Aside from the misspelling of a Beanie Baby's name, other common misprints are poem variations, grammatical errors and birthday variations. Tusk is the only Beanie Baby found with four different poem variations. According to Ty, Tusk's poem should read:

"Tusk brushes his teeth everyday
To keep them shiny, it's the only way
Teeth are special, so you must try
And they will sparkle when you say "Hi"!"

In addition to this version, Tusk has also been found with these poem endings:

-So they sparkle when You say "Hi"!
-So they will sparkle when you say "Hi"!
-To sparkle when you say "Hi"!

Sparky, the dalmatian, is another Beanie Baby with several endings to his poem. Ty lists his poem as:

"Sparky rides proud on the fire truck
Ringing the bell and pushing his luck
Gets under foot when trying to help
He often gets stepped on and lets out a yelp!"

Sparky has also been found with these poem endings:

-He often gets stepped on crying yelp!
-Step on him and he'll let out a yelp!

The biggest source of tag misprints is grammatical or typographical errors. In some instances the tags will be incorrect for one production run, and then corrected on the next production run, vice versa, or are never corrected at all. A well-known example of a grammatical error is the line of Garcia's poem that says: "The Beanies use to follow him around" instead of "used to." Then there is Squealer's poem that at one time read: Squealer "like" to joke around. When this was corrected on later tags to "likes", an error was made in the last line: "There is no doubt he'll will make you smile!"

Other examples of typographical or grammatical errors are: Chops' poem where surely is spelled "surly"; Hoot's poem where quite is spelled "qutie"; Scottie's tag where always is spelled "slways"; Bones with "Your" instead of You're; and Chocolate with moose spelled rnoose (with r and n instead of the letter m).

It has often been thought that some Beanie Babies have a misprinted birthday, because at one time or other the date on the tag did not match the birthday list that Ty put out. Actually, there are only two Beanie Babies that have more than one birthday printed on their swing tag. Freckles can be found with the dates - 7/28/96 or 6/3/96, and Scottie can be found with the dates - 6/15/96 or 6/3/96. See page 63.

Tush Tags: (body tags)

One of the more notable tush tag misprints occurred when Libearty was first released, and on its tush tag the word Beanie was misspelled "Beanine". The misspelling was eventually corrected, but not until after the market had been fairly saturated with the Beanine Libearty. While the Beanine misspelling is sought after by collectors, and is helpful in dating whether Libearty was produced earlier versus later in 1996, it is thought that Libearty with "Beanie" spelled correctly may actually be the more rare of the two.

Another misspelling occurred on the tush tag of **all** Beanies that were in production in mid-1996. On the tush tag, "surface washable" is spelled "sufrace washable."

Due to the high volume of Beanie Babies being produced at factories in China and Korea, a large number of Beanie Babies have been allowed to leave the factory with manufacturing defects. Some of these are quite minor such as eyes slightly misplaced, or missing whiskers. Others can be quite noticeable such as Beanie Babies completely missing body parts like eyes, noses, legs; or parts wrongly attached such as ears, legs and even wings put on backwards.

Some of the Beanie Baby oddities collectors have found are extremely unique.

Lizzy with a striped tail

Libearty with the flag sewn on upside down

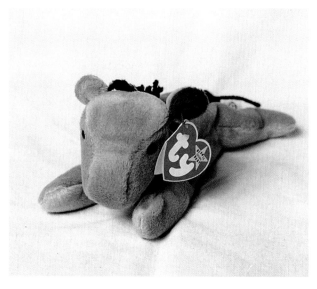

Derby with his ear on backwards

Inky with 9 legs instead of 8 legs

MANUFACTURING ODDITIES

Quackers without eyes or eyebrows

Quackers with his wing on backwards

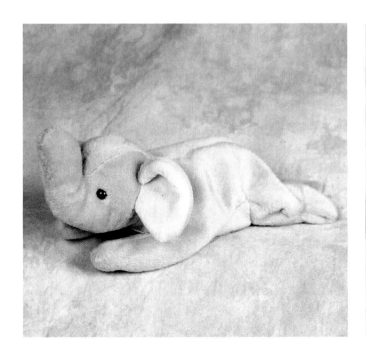

Righty without a flag

Lefty without a flag

Stripes with fuzzy belly (left)

Daisy without a spot

Spot with an all white face

Stripes with the stripes running lengthwise (bottom) instead of around the body

There are several tag "cover-ups" that have appeared on the Ty swing tags since Beanie Babies were first introduced. It appears that when a need arose to change information on a particular tag, rather than throw out what was in stock, Ty printed up small stickers with the correct information, and covered up the old information.

The earliest evidence of such a cover-up appears on numerous first version heart tags that have Ty Inc. information covered up with Ty (UK) LTD information.*1 This practice was discontinued when the second version heart tags were produced, providing each country with their own individual tag.*2 Another instance of a tag cover-up occurred on some of the old-face Teddies. Ty used already printed heart tags that said "Made in China", and covered the words with stickers saying "Made in Korea."*3

The next instance of a tag cover-up appeared on Bongo the monkey early in 1995. It appears that Ty originally planned on calling Bongo by the name of "Nana", and then decided to change it to Bongo. Since tags were already printed up saying "Nana™ style 4067", small stickers were printed saying, "Bongo™ style 4067" and placed over Nana's name and style number. A few tags, however, did make it into circulation with the name Nana uncovered.*4

The largest tag cover-up concerns Ty's web site. Beginning in 1996, Ty had the web site "http://www.ty.com" printed on the Beanie Babies' swing tags. However, at the time that the tags were printed, Ty did not have the rights to the www.ty.com domain name, as it had been granted in early January to a business called Tech Yard. In late January, Ty offered to buy the domain name from Tech Yard, but the gentleman who was using it refused to give it up. Then Ty sued, and the case turned to the courts with Ty defending his claim that Ty was a registered trademark. Ty eventually won the case.

However, until the case was legally settled, Ty had to cover up the www.ty.com web page address on their tags. It is not uncommon to find tags with the web site covered up with specially cut white stickers, or with the web site completely cut off the bottom of the tag. For a brief period during the summer, when the first set of tags were depleted, and the case was still unresolved, newly printed tags either said "visit our web page!" with no address given, or there was no mention of a web page whatsoever. Tags without the web site, or with the web site covered up, appear on Beanie Babies that were in production mid-1996. The first web site cover-up appeared on Libearty. Originally Libearty's date of birth read "Summer Olympics 1996." Due to possible copyright infringement the word "Olympics" was covered up as well as the web site.

Website and Olympics covered up	Website tag bottom cut off	Tag with "Visit our web page!!!"	Tag with no mention of website.

*1-3   See Ty Heart Tags page 70.
*4   See Nana page 45.

On Friday, April 11, 1997, McDonald's introduced Teenie Beanies, a miniature version of the full-sized Beanie Babies made by Ty, Inc., in their Happy Meals.

As April 11th approached, McDonald's realized that they had seriously underestimated the number of toys that were going to be needed. They hoped to avert the problem by taking a "low key" approach in advertising. Instead of a "Big Mac sized" advertising campaign like the company used in other promotions, McDonald's had only in-store displays, which weren't put up until the day the promotion started. They commissioned only three 30-second "mini" TV commercials, which aired on a limited basis starting the day before the promotion.

Despite ordering 100 million toys, McDonald's underestimated the demand and high collectibility of these toys; a direct result of the Beanie Baby frenzy sweeping the country. Individual restaurants reported sales of Happy Meals at 6 to 10 times the normal rate and many were entirely sold out of Teenie Beanies within the first week.

By the end of the first week, McDonald's announced that the promotion would officially end April 25th, three weeks early, and issued a national public apology in the form of TV and radio commercials, as well as full-page newspaper ads.

TEENIE BEANIES

Description

The Teenie Beanie promotion featured 10 animals which were intended to be released two per week, for 5 weeks, in the following order: #1 Patti, #2 Pinky, #3 Chops, #4 Chocolate, #5 Goldie, #6 Speedy, #7 Seamore, #8 Snort, #9 Quacks and #10 Lizz.

These miniature Teenie Beanies are made of a polyester velour, and are filled with plastic pellets and stuffing. Their facial features are embroidered on, making this toy safe even for very young children. Each Teenie Beanie came individually packaged in a clear plastic bag with its name and item # on it.

Patti the Platypus is a fuchsia colored platypus. She has a yellowish-gold beak, yellowish-gold feet and black eyes.

Pinky the Flamingo is a bright pink flamingo with pale pink legs. She has an orange beak, two-tone wings and black eyes. The topside of her wings is made out of the same plush material as the Beanie Babies.

Chops the Lamb is a cream-colored lamb with a black face and two-tone ears. He has a pink nose and blue eyes.

Chocolate the Moose is a brown moose with orange antlers and black eyes.

Goldie the Fish is an orange fish with black eyes and two rows of orange stitching on each fin.

Speedy the Turtle is a green turtle with black eyes and a brown shell consisting of darker brown spots "flocked" onto a lighter brown background.

Seamore the Seal is a white seal with a black nose, eyes and eyebrows.

Snort the Bull is a red bull with cream-colored horns, two-tone ears, black eyes and two black nostrils that are sewn onto his cream-colored snout.

Quacks the Duck is a yellow duck with black eyes and eyebrows. He has an orange beak and orange feet. The top side of his wings is made of the same plush material as the Beanie Babies.

Lizz the Lizard is a dark blue lizard with black spots scattered on top of her body and a solid orange belly. She has a red felt forked tongue and black eyes.

During initial design stages, several prototypes of each Teenie Beanie were made. From those prototypes the final selection of the Teenie Beanie that was to be part of the McDonald's promotion, was chosen. Listed on each prototype is the production number and the design approval date.
Example: Pinky the Flamingo has the following information listed
on the prototype: 11834.PF.OO2 8.16

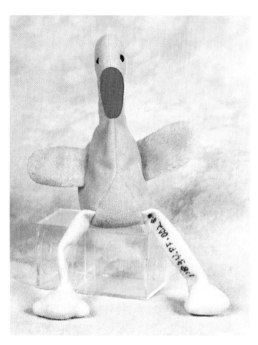 

Pinky the flamingo

This Pinky prototype (left) is larger in size, is a lighter pink color and has a red beak. The prototype information is written on its left leg.

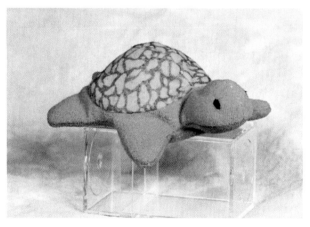 

Speedy the turtle

This Speedy prototype (left) has the same body design as the Teenie Beanie, but the shell is green and covered with a yellowish green pattern. The eyes are stitched vertically in contrast to the horizontal stitching on the Teenie Beanie. The prototype information is written on its bottom.

Chocolate the Moose

This Chocolate prototype (right) has the same body design as the Teenie Beanie, but the color of the body and antlers are slightly darker. The eyes are stitched vertically in contrast to the horizontally stitched eyes on the Teenie Beanie. The prototype information is written on its bottom.

Seamore the Seal

This Seamore prototype (right) is slightly larger in size than the Teenie Beanie. It is a duller white color and its facial features are more pronounced. The prototype information is written on its bottom.

Tush Tags: (body tags)

The Teenie Beanies were produced for McDonald's through their own manufacturing sources, under the terms of a licensing agreement with Ty, Inc. Ty had no involvement or responsibility in the manufacture and distribution of Teenie Beanies. McDonald's contracted with two different companies to produce the Teenie Beanies - Simon Marketing Inc., in Los Angeles, California and MB Sales in Westmont, Illinois.

Having two manufacturers of the Teenie Beanies accounts for the differences found in the tush tags. Simon Marketing produced five of the Teenie Beanies - Pinky, Chops, Chocolate, Speedy, and Seamore. Their tags have red printing on one side of the tag and black on the other. MB Sales produced the other five - Pattie, Goldie, Snort, Quacks, and Lizz. Some of their tags have black printing on both sides, and some red printing on one side of the tag and black on the other. All of the Teenie Beanie tush tags have "©1993 TY INC." on the front and "©1996 McDonald's Corp." on the back. Some of the tags also have code numbers stamped on them. These refer to production bag and tag numbering sequences.

Teenie Beanies produced exclusively for Canada have slightly larger tush tags, and have the additional black and white tush tag with the manufacturer's information printed in both French and English.

Heart Tag: (swing tag)

Attached by red thread to each Teenie Beanie is a single sided Ty heart tag similar to the third version heart tag found on Beanie Babies. The backside of the tag bears the trademark "Teenie Beanie Babies ™/MC" and the individual Teenie Beanie's name.

Collectible Ranking

Teenie Beanies ranked according to availability:

4 star = hardest to find; 1 star = easiest to find

Pinky	★★★★
Patti	★★★
Chops	★★★
Chocolate	★★★
Snort	★★
Seamore	★★
Lizz	★★
Quacks	★★
Speedy	★
Goldie	★

This button was given to McDonald's employees after the Teenie Beanies' promotion.

After the filming of the three McDonald's "mini" commercials was completed, several production items were donated for an auction to be held at McDonald's annual convention on May 3, 1997, in St. Louis, Missouri. Proceeds of the auction were donated to Ronald McDonald House Charities. The items donated included the three original storyboard drawings, all signed by the artist; the production book made by the film company, which included scripts and storyboards; the 3-D Teenie Beanie Logo; black and white printouts of scenes from the commercial; photoboards of the finished commercials; color photos of the Beanie logo; color photocopies of the original designs of the 10 Teenie Beanies; an audio cassette of the commercials' music; and a videotape of the finished commercials.

These are color photocopies of the original designs of the 10 Teenie Beanies.

TEENY BEANIES

Patti Platypus

TEENY BEANIES

Pinky Flamingo

TEENY BEANIES

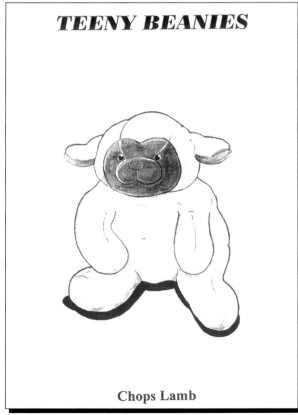

Chops Lamb

TEENY BEANIES

Chocolate Moose

TEENIE BEANIE RENDERINGS

TEENY BEANIES

Goldie Goldfish

TEENY BEANIES

Speedy Turtle

TEENY BEANIES

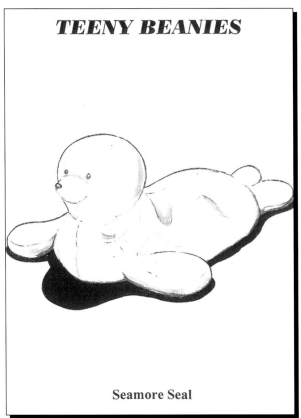

Seamore Seal

TEENY BEANIES

Snort

~~Tabasco Red Bull~~

TEENY BEANIES

Quackers Duck

TEENY BEANIES

Lizzy Lizard

ℬeanie Babies Collectible Ranking

Brownie, the brown bear ★★★★★
Nana, the monkey with tan tail - b/w tush tag ★★★★★
Patti, the deep fuchsia platypus ★★★★★
Peanut, the royal blue elephant ★★★★★
Punchers, the red lobster ★★★★★
Quacker, the duck without wings ★★★★★
Quacke<u>r</u>s, the duck without wings ★★★★★
Spot, the black and white dog without a spot ★★★★★
Zip, the all black cat with pink ears (no white) ★★★★★

Chilly, the white polar bear ★★★★
Derby, the fine-mane horse ★★★★
Humphrey, the camel ★★★★
Nip, the all gold cat with pink ears (no white) ★★★★
Patti, the magenta platypus ★★★★
Patti, the raspberry platypus ★★★★
Peking, the panda bear ★★★★
Teddy, the new face-teal bear ★★★★
Teddy, the new face-violet bear ★★★★
Teddy, the old face-brown bear ★★★★

Bronty, the brontosaurus ★★★
Flutter, the tie-dyed butterfly ★★★
Lizzy, the tie-dyed lizard ★★★
Quacker, the duck with wings ★★★
Slither, the snake ★★★
Teddy, the new face-cranberry bear ★★★
Teddy, the new face-jade bear ★★★
Teddy, the new face-magenta bear ★★★
Teddy, the old face-cranberry bear ★★★
Web, the spider ★★★

Digger, the orange crab ★★
Happy, the gray hippo ★★
Inky, the tan octopus with a mouth ★★
Inky, the tan octopus without a mouth ★★
Maple/Pride, the white bear with Canadian flag ★★
Nip, the gold cat with white face and belly ★★
Rex, the tyrannosaurus ★★
Spook, the ghost ★★
Steg, the stegosaurus ★★
Teddy, the old face-jade bear ★★
Teddy, the old face-magenta bear ★★
Teddy, the old face-teal bear ★★
Teddy, the old face-violet bear ★★
Trap, the mouse ★★
Zip, the black cat with white face and belly ★★

5 Stars = most rare; 1 Star = least rare

Bongo, the monkey with brown tail - r/w tush tag / no name	★
Bongo, the monkey with tan tail - b/w tush tag	★
Bongo, the monkey with tan tail - r/w tush tag / no name	★
Bubbles, the black and yellow fish	★
Bumble, the bee	★
Caw, the crow	★
Chops, the lamb	★
Coral, the tie-dyed fish	★
Digger, the red crab	★
Flash, the dolphin	★
Garcia, the tie-dyed bear	★
Grunt, the razorback hog	★
Inch, the inchworm with felt antennae	★
Kiwi, the toucan	★
Lefty, the donkey with American flag	★
Libearty, the white bear with American flag	★
Libearty/Beanine, the white bear with American flag	★
Lucky, the ladybug with 7 felt dots	★
Manny, the manatee	★
Mystic, the fine-mane unicorn	★
Radar, the bat	★
Righty, the elephant with American flag	★
Sly, the brown-belly fox	★
Sparky, the dalmatian	★
Splash, the orca whale	★
Sting, the ray	★
Stripes, the black and orange tiger	★
Tabasco, the red bull	★
Tank, the 7-line armadillo	★
Tank, the 9-line armadillo	★
Tuck, the walrus	★
Tusk, the walrus	★

Ty, Inc. and the Chicago Cubs "teamed" up for the first ever Beanie Baby giveaway that was held on Sunday, May 18, 1997. Beanie Baby "Cubbie" was given away to the first 10,000 children, age 13 and under, who entered Wrigley Field. In addition, each child received a promotional certificate with their Cubbie Beanie Baby, compliments of the Chicago Cubs and Pepsi who sponsored Beanie Babies' Day.

The promotion drew a season-high crowd of 37,958, with fans lining up hours before the game. Ty Warner threw out the first ball and, with the help of two home runs by Sammy Sosa, the Cubs held on for a 5-3 victory over the San Francisco Giants. "Cubbie" was truly a good luck charm for the Cubs.

Chicago Cubs Commemorative Card

In August of 1996, the Ty Co. started the "Beanie Baby Guestbook" internet site (www. ty.com). The Ty Guestbook offered a site where people could communicate with other Beanie Baby collectors from all over the world. In time, other Beanie Baby web sites were created, and collectors were able to buy, sell and trade retired Beanie Babies online. These web sites helped to increase awareness of retired Beanie Babies as a collectible. Soon, demand for retired Beanie Babies surged, and so did the prices.

During September 1996, we were able to compile reliable price data for the first time, thanks in part to the increasing amount of price quotes on the various web sites. Our price data is also based on our own trading activity, both online and at collectors' shows. The following chart starts with September 1996 price data, for retired Beanie Babies that were being actively traded at that time.

The second column of price data is for December 1996. During the period between September and December, many people were completing their collection and prices for most of the "reasonably" priced Beanie Babies were stable. One notable exception was for Teddy, whose prices increased for all 11 of its styles.

At the same time, some significant price decreases occurred for some of the more expensive Beanie Babies, such as Peanut, the royal blue elephant; Zip, the all black cat; Patti, the raspberry platypus; Quacker/Quackers, the wingless duck; and Spot, the dog without a spot. Peanut dropped from $800 to as low as $500. Zip dropped from a September peak of $500 down to a low of $325. Raspberry Patti dropped from $750 to $550. Quacker/Quackers and Spot fell from $1,000 to $750. Other examples include Chilly, Peking, and Slither, who went down in value from $300 to $200.

During this period, collectors were unwilling to pay premium prices for these Beanie Babies because of a prevailing uncertainty about the longevity of the Beanie Baby collection, and concern about values dropping. This uncertainty was due in part to a slower than anticipated 1996 Christmas season. Approaching the Christmas holidays, collectors were sure that the retired Beanie Baby market would be "red hot," but it just didn't happen! There was still buying, selling and trading going on, but it was slow! Many collectors became worried that the market for retired Beanie Babies was going to collapse.

Adding to the uncertainty was a rumor that Ty Warner was going to introduce 13 new Beanie Babies, as well as retire up to 13 others. A fear of an oversupply and too many types of Beanie Babies crept into the market. Everyone wondered how this was going to impact the secondary market. Collectors were scared and prices started to come down for the higher priced, hard to find Beanie Babies.

During December, the market was very quiet. Adding to the problem, the Ty Guestbook web site was not accessible during the last half of December, because it was being upgraded. There were a few other Beanie Baby web sites to visit, but the volume of collector postings was down dramatically. Fortunately, this situation wouldn't last long - due to the power of the Internet!

MARKET TREND ANALYSIS

Determined Beanie Baby fans began searching for new Beanie Baby related web sites, so they could continue to get information and conduct trading activity. As a result, web sites such as "BeanieMom," "Kim's Auction" and "Collector's Corner" became popular. Kim's site was pivotal in increasing the awareness of retired Beanie Babies as a collectible. Tapping into the incredible marketing potential of the Internet, Kim ingeniously linked her site with a variety of other collector web sites. Suddenly, collectors that were previously unaware of Beanie Babies joined in the hunt and Beanie mania was on again! By the middle of January, the Internet "quiet" period was over and the demand for retired Beanie Babies was greater than ever before!

Sparking further interest, Ty Warner used the Internet to make the first ever public announcement of which Beanie Babies were to be retired and which new ones were to be introduced in early 1997. The Ty Guestbook displayed an ad, during its dormant period in late December, that this announcement would be made, and the Ty Guestbook would become active again, on January 1, 1997, at 12 noon.

The Beanie Baby web pages, as well as the retail stores, were buzzing with excitement! Which Beanie Babies were going to be retired? Everyone waited with great anticipation for the January 1st announcement. Just before 12 noon, thousands of collectors were on the Ty Guestbook site, waiting for this important news . We all waited, and waited, and waited but the promised announcement was not there. Nine hours later, around 9:00 p.m., the news was finally posted - on the BeanieMom web site.

During January 1997, the focus of which retired Beanie Babies people were now buying began to change! New collectors, who did not have any of the older Beanie Babies to trade or sell, had to start from rock bottom. There were very few, if any, of the retired Beanie Babies left on the store shelves to buy or use for trade. Purchases had to occur in the secondary market. These new collectors started by acquiring the lower priced retired Beanie Babies, those below $100.00. These included Bronty, Bumble, Caw, Flutter, Inch, Rex, Steg, Stripes, Tank, Web, etc. Due to strong demand, the prices of most of these "reasonably" priced retired Beanie Babies doubled or tripled by the third week of January 1997.

The 1997 "newly" retired Beanie Babies (Chops, Coral, Kiwi, Lefty, Libearty, Righty, Sting, Tabasco, and Tusk) were also in great demand. Store shelves were being cleaned out as more and more collectors joined in on the Beanie Baby mania!

At the same time, the "new" 1997 Beanie Babies (Bernie, Crunch, Doby, Fleece, Floppity, Gracie, Hippity, Hoppity, Mel, Nuts, Pouch, Snip, and Snort) were starting to arrive in stores and people were buying them like there was no tomorrow. Merchants couldn't keep enough Beanie Babies in stock; their shelves were being emptied as fast as they could fill them.

Prices of the retired Beanie Babies continued to escalate, as more collectors searched relentlessly, outbidding others at high prices just so they could complete their collections. As shown on the chart, prices for almost all of the Beanie Babies had increased by February, and many of the more expensive ones were back up near their September value levels.

The frenzy on the Beanie Baby web boards accelerated during February when word leaked out that McDonald's was producing 10 smaller versions of Beanie Babies, called "Teenie Beanies", for a "Happy Meal" promotion. This promotion began on April 11th, and as we all know by now, it was the most successful toy giveaway in history! McDonald's gave away 100 million Teenie Babies in less than two weeks!

If people hadn't heard about Beanie Babies before the McDonald's promotion, they sure did now! It even caught Wall Street's attention, with articles about Beanie Babies being written in prominent business publications, such as the Wall Street Journal, Investor's Business Daily and Barron's. A new group of collectors joined the mania as a result of the Teenie Beanies campaign, and secondary market prices were on the upward climb again.

Ty, Inc. kept the excitement going, when word spread that they were going to retire 9 more Beanie Babies, and introduce 14 new ones, on May 11th (Mother's Day). Once again, their internet site would be used for this announcement. However, there was no specific time promised. To everyone's surprise, the list of the new introductions and retirements unfolded on the Guestbook site, just after 12 midnight.

Repeating the shopping scene after the January 1st announcement, collectors headed out to the stores to buy newly retired Beanie Babies. This time, however, the search was in vain for most people. Store shelves were bare and there were very few Beanie Babies to be found. This scarcity was partially due to a cutback in the supply pipeline from Ty, Inc. During the middle of March, Ty began limiting their retail customers to a maximum allotment of 36 of each Beanie Baby a month. In addition, Ty announced that they would not fill some backorders. One of the reasons for the supply quotas being imposed was due to increased demand for Beanie Babies in Canada, the United Kingdom and new market areas that opened up across the United States.

Because of supply limitations, the price of the May 11th retired Beanie Babies quickly shot up to the level of the January 1st retirements. Even the current $5.00 Beanie Babies were being sold on the secondary market as soon as they left the stores - for $15.00 to $25.00 each!

The chart on the following pages summarizes the escalation in prices. The events reported above, starting in August, 1996, all contributed to the demand and price momentum. As of the date of this writing (November, 1997), record new high price levels have recently been reached.

In order to keep abreast of ongoing trends in Beanie Baby market values, we recommend that you regularly check our Market Analysis and Pricing Guide found on the BeanieMom web site (http://www.beaniemom.com). Our Price Guide is updated every Monday, and is your best source for current price information. Also, you may want to subscribe to our semi-monthy newsletter — "Beanie Mania Bulletin" (see order form in the back of our book).

MARKET TREND ANALYSIS

Beanie Name	Mid Sept 1996	Mid Dec 1996	Mid Feb 1997	Mid March 1997	Mid April 1997	Mid May 1997	Mid June 1997	Mid July 1997	Mid August 1997	Mid Sept. 1997	Mid October 1997
Bongo, brown tail-r/w tush tag-no name				$75-100	$75-100	$75-100	$75-100	$50-75	$50-75	$50-75	$50-75
Bongo, tan tail-b/w tush tag					$125-150	$125-150	$125-150	$100-125	$100-125	$100-125	$100-125
Bongo, tan tail-r/w tush tag-no name					$20-25	$20-25	$20-25	$25-40	$25-40	$35-50	$35-50
Bronty	$30-35	$35-50	$100-125	$300-350	$400-500	$400-500	$350-450	$375-450	$375-450	$400-450	$450-550
Brownie				$500-800	$500-800	$700-1,000	$600-800	$800-1,200	$800-1,200	$850-1,200	$1,000-1,300
Bubbles						$25-50	$25-50	$25-40	$25-40	$35-50	$45-60
Bumble (3rd generation tag)	$20-25	$25-30	$40-45	$100-125	$125-175	$125-200	$125-175	$150-200	$175-225	$250-300	$300-350
Bumble (4th generation tag)							$175-225	$175-225	$200-250	$275-325	$350-400
Caw	$30-35	$35-40	$50-60	$100-125	$125-175	$150-200	$150-200	$175-225	$200-250	$275-325	$325-400
Chilly	$300	$200	$225-275	$350-450	$600-700	$600-800	$600-800	$600-800	$725-825	$775-875	$850-950
Chops			$20-30	$25-35	$40-50	$45-60	$45-60	$40-60	$45-60	$45-65	$60-80
Coral			$10-15	$25-30	$30-40	$45-60	$45-60	$45-60	$45-60	$50-70	$65-85
Derby, fine-mane				$50-100	$150-200	$200-350	$300-450	$350-450	$350-450	$400-450	$500-600
Digger, orange	$65-75	$65-75	$75-100	$150-200	$200-250	$250-350	$250-350	$250-350	$275-350	$325-375	$350-450
Digger, red						$25-50	$30-50	$25-40	$25-40	$35-50	$40-55
Dino Set (Bronty, Rex and Steg)	$70-75	$85-95	$150-200	$450-650	$750-850	$800-900	$750-850	$750-850	$825-925	$875-975	$1,000-1,300
Doodle										$25-50	$30-45
Flash						$25-50	$30-50	$25-45	$25-45	$30-40	$40-55
Flutter	$30-40	$50-65	$75-100	$300-450	$400-500	$400-500	$350-450	$350-450	$425-475	$450-500	$500-600
Garcia					$50-75	$50-100	$50-75	$50-75	$40-75	$45-65	$50-70
Grunt					$45-55	$25-50	$50-75	$45-75	$50-75	$65-80	$85-115
Happy, gray	$65-75	$65-75	$75-90	$150-200	$200-250	$250-350	$250-350	$250-350	$275-350	$325-375	$325-450
Humphrey	$125-150	$150-175	$200-250	$550-650	$700-900	$700-900	$800-900	$750-900	$800-900	$800-900	$850-1,000
Inch, felt antennae	$10-15	$10-15	$15-20	$35-50	$50-75	$50-75	$50-75	$50-75	$65-85	$65-85	$85-110
Inky, tan with mouth	$65-75	$65-75	$75-90	$150-200	$200-250	$225-325	$200-300	$200-300	$225-300	$300-350	$350-450
Inky, tan without mouth	$65-75	$65-75	$100-125	$175-225	$225-275	$250-350	$250-350	$250-350	$275-350	$325-375	$400-500
Kiwi			$15-20	$25-35	$35-45	$40-50	$40-60	$45-60	$45-60	$60-80	$65-90
Lefty			$10-15	$25-30	$35-45	$50-75	$50-75	$50-75	$65-85	$75-100	$90-115
Libearty			$15-20	$25-35	$40-50	$60-80	$60-80	$60-80	$65-85	$80-100	$100-125
Libearty/Beanine			$20-25	$30-40	$45-55	$55-75	$55-75	$55-75	$60-75	$75-100	$95-115
Lizzy, tie-dyed	$150-175	$150-175	$125-175	$250-350	$350-400	$350-400	$350-400	$350-400	$375-425	$400-450	$400-500
Lucky, 7 felt dots	$15-50	$15-50	$25-35	$50-90	$75-100	$50-75	$40-60	$40-60	$65-85	$65-85	$85-110
Lucky, 21 dots										$150-200	$275-375
Manny						$25-50	$40-60	$45-60	$50-75	$60-85	$85-110
Maple/Pride				$75-150	$150-200	$175-225	$175-225	$200-250	$225-275	$300-350	$350-450
Mystic, fine-mane				$55-75	$75-125	$100-150	$100-150	$100-150	$100-150	$100-150	$100-150
Nana, tan tail - b/w tush tag					$600-800	$600-800	$600-800	$800-1,200	$800-1,200	$850-1,200	$900-1,300
Nip, all gold	$300-350	$300-350	$300-350	$400-500	$425-525	$500-600	$500-600	$500-600	$500-600	$550-650	$650-750
Nip, gold, white face and belly	$75-80	$80-95	$80-95	$150-200	$150-200	$175-225	$175-225	$150-200	$200-250	$225-275	$275-350
Patti, deep fuchsia							$600-800	$600-800	$600-800	$600-800	$650-850

Beanie Name	Mid Sept 1996	Mid Dec 1996	Mid Feb 1997	Mid March 1997	Mid April 1997	Mid May 1997	Mid June 1997	Mid July 1997	Mid August 1997	Mid Sept. 1997	Mid October 1997
Patti, magenta	$550-600	$500-550	$450-600	$450-600	$450-600	$450-600	$400-500	$400-500	$450-550	$450-550	$500-600
Patti, raspberry	$750	$550-600	$550-700	$550-700	$550-700	$550-700	$450-600	$450-600	$550-650	$550-650	$600-700
Peanut, royal blue	$775-800	$500-550	$475-750	$700-1,000	$900-1,200	$900-1,200	$1,000-1,400	$1,000-1,400	$1,100-1,500	$1,400-1,800	$1,700-2,100
Peking	$300	$200	$225-275	$400-500	$500-600	$500-700	$500-650	$500-650	$600-700	$675-775	$800-900
Punchers	$1,000						$800-1,000	$750-1,000	$800-1,000	$800-1,000	$850-1,000
Quacker/Quackers, without wings		$750	$750-1,000	$750-1,000	$900-1,200	$900-1,200	$900-1,200	$900-1,200	$900-1,200	$1,000-1,200	$1,100-1,300
Radar						$50-75	$40-60	$40-60	$50-65	$50-70	$65-90
Rex	$25-30	$25-30	$40-60	$150-200	$175-225	$200-250	$175-225	$175-250	$225-275	$250-300	$325-400
Righty			$10-15	$25-30	$35-45	$50-75	$50-65	$50-75	$65-85	$75-100	$90-115
Slither	$300	$200	$200-250	$375-450	$500-600	$500-600	$500-600	$500-600	$550-650	$600-700	$750-900
Sly, brown-belly	$10-15	$10-15	$15-25	$50-75	$75-125	$75-125	$50-75	$50-75	$75-100	$75-100	$75-100
Sparky						$35-50	$35-50	$25-40	$35-45	$35-50	$45-60
Splash						$25-50	$30-50	$25-45	$25-45	$30-40	$45-55
Spook					$150-200	$150-200	$150-200	$100-150	$100-150	$100-150	$125-175
Spot, without a spot	$1,000	$750	$750-1,000	$750-1,000	$900-1,200	$900-1,200	$900-1,200	$900-1,200	$1,000-1,300	$1,000-1,300	$1,000-1,300
Steg	$20-25	$20-25	$55-75	$150-225	$200-250	$250-350	$250-350	$250-350	$250-350	$300-350	$350-450
Sting			$15-25	$25-35	$40-50	$45-55	$45-60	$45-65	$50-65	$60-75	$75-100
Stripes, black and orange	$15-20	$15-20	$25-30	$65-100	$100-150	$150-200	$150-200	$150-200	$150-200	$175-225	$200-250
Tabasco			$25-50	$75-125	$75-125	$125-175	$100-150	$125-175	$125-175	$130-180	$125-175
Tank, 7-line	$15-20	$15-20	$25-30	$40-75	$50-75	$50-75	$50-75	$50-75	$65-85	$65-85	$100-125
Tank, 9-line	$10-15	$10-15	$20-25	$40-75	$50-75	$50-75	$75-100	$75-100	$85-100	$75-90	$100-150
Teddy, new face-cranberry	$75-100	$100-125	$125-175	$200-250	$350-450	$400-500	$400-500	$400-500	$450-550	$500-600	$650-850
Teddy, new face-jade	$75-100	$100-125	$125-175	$200-250	$350-450	$400-500	$400-500	$400-500	$450-550	$500-600	$650-850
Teddy, new face-magenta	$75-100	$100-125	$125-175	$200-250	$350-450	$400-500	$400-500	$400-500	$450-550	$500-600	$650-850
Teddy, new face-teal	$100-150	$150-200	$350-400	$450-550	$550-650	$550-650	$550-650	$550-650	$600-700	$700-800	$800-1,000
Teddy, new face-violet	$100-150	$150-200	$300-350	$400-500	$500-600	$500-600	$500-600	$500-600	$600-700	$700-800	$800-1,000
Teddy, old face-brown	$75-100	$100-125	$150-175	$225-275	$350-500	$550-650	$550-650	$550-650	$600-700	$650-750	$800-1,000
Teddy, old face-cranberry	$75-100	$100-125	$125-175	$200-250	$350-500	$500-600	$500-600	$500-600	$550-650	$650-750	$700-900
Teddy, old face-jade	$75-100	$100-125	$125-175	$175-225	$250-350	$300-400	$350-450	$350-450	$400-500	$450-550	$600-800
Teddy, old face-magenta	$75-100	$100-125	$125-175	$175-225	$250-350	$275-350	$300-400	$300-400	$400-500	$450-550	$600-800
Teddy, old face-teal	$75-100	$100-125	$125-175	$175-225	$300-400	$300-400	$300-400	$300-400	$400-500	$450-550	$600-800
Teddy, old face-violet	$75-100	$100-125	$125-175	$175-225	$300-400	$300-400	$350-450	$350-450	$450-550	$500-600	$600-800
Trap	$125-150	$125-150	$125-150	$175-250	$350-450	$400-500	$350-450	$400-500	$425-500	$450-525	$550-650
Tuck			$20-30	$30-40	$35-45	$45-55	$45-55	$45-55	$45-55	$50-60	$70-90
Tusk			$15-25	$25-30	$30-40	$40-50	$40-50	$40-50	$40-50	$45-55	$60-75
Web	$45-50	$50-75	$75-100	$300-450	$550-650	$550-650	$450-550	$450-550	$500-600	$525-625	$600-700
Zip, all black	$350-500	$325-450	$400-750	$600-1,000	$900-1,200	$900-1,200	$900-1,200	$900-1,200	$1,000-1,300	$1,000-1,300	$1,000-1,300
Zip, black, white face and belly	$80-85	$85-100	$85-100	$175-225	$175-225	$200-250	$175-225	$175-225	$225-275	$250-300	$300-375

Prices are not listed, if a Beanie Baby was not retired at that time, its existence was unknown or if there was not a separate price for that particular Beanie Baby variation during that time period. The prices of the October 1, 1997 newly retired Beanie Babies are listed on page 136.

MARKET TREND ANALYSIS

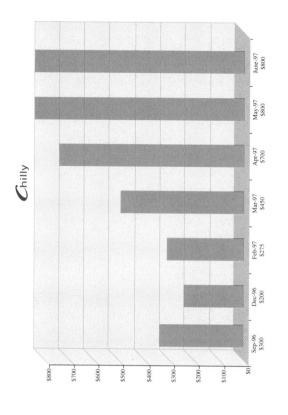

Chilly

Sep-96	$300
Dec-96	$200
Feb-97	$275
Mar-97	$450
Apr-97	$700
May-97	$800
June-97	$800

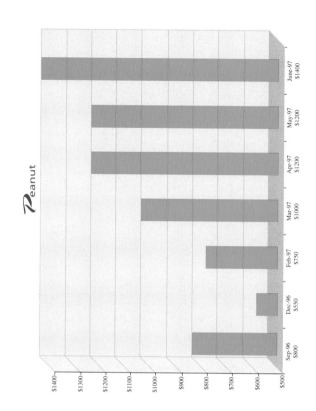

Peanut

Sep-96	$800
Dec-96	$550
Feb-97	$750
Mar-97	$1000
Apr-97	$1200
May-97	$1200
June-97	$1400

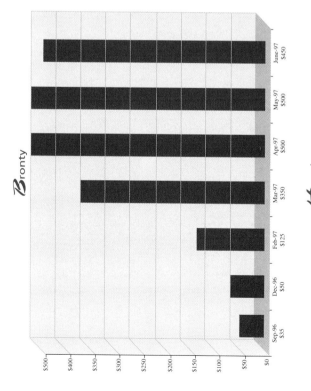

Bronty

Sep-96	$35
Dec-96	$50
Feb-97	$125
Mar-97	$350
Apr-97	$500
May-97	$500
June-97	$450

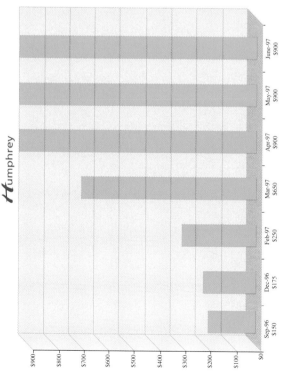

Humphrey

Sep-96	$150
Dec-96	$175
Feb-97	$250
Mar-97	$650
Apr-97	$900
May-97	$900
June-97	$900

These bar graphs represent the price fluctuation for Bronty, the brontosaurus; Chilly, the polar bear; Humphrey, the camel; and Peanut, the royal blue elephant from September 1996 to June 1997.

PPENDI

1988

1989

1990

1991

1992 Collection

1992

1993 Collection

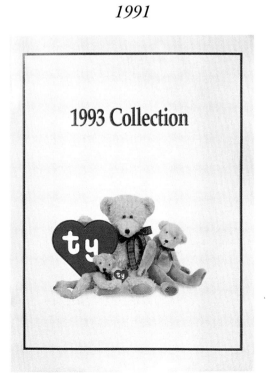

1993

Beanie Babies were first introduced in this 1994 catalog.

NEW INTRODUCTIONS

Courtesy of Bears by the Sea, Pismo Beach, California

Courtesy of Ted E. Bear Shoppe of Florida

TY TAGS FILL-IN CHART

Style No	Beanie Name	Hang Tags				1993 b/w	1995 b/w	1993 red NO Name	1995 red No Name	1993 red WITH Name	1995 red WITH Name	1996 red WITH Name	Can b/w	Korea/China
		1st	2nd	3rd	4th									
4032	Ally													
4074	Baldy													
4109	Bernie													
4009	Bessie													
4011	Blackie													
4163	Blizzard													
4001	Bones													
4067	Bongo-brown tail													
4067	Bongo-tan tail													
4085	Bronty													
4010	Brownie													
4078	Bubbles													
4016	Bucky													
4045	Bumble													
4071	Caw													
4012	Chilly													
4121	Chip													
4015	Chocolate													
4019	Chops													
4083	Claude													
4160	Congo													
4079	Coral													
4130	Crunch													
4010	Cubbie													
4052	Curly													
4006	Daisy													
4008	Derby-coarse-mane													
4008	Derby-fine-mane													
4027	Digger-orange													
4027	Digger-red													
4110	Doby													
4171	Doodle													
4100	Dotty													
4018	Ears													
4180	Echo													

Style No	Beanie Name	Hang Tags 1st	2nd	3rd	4th	1993 b/w	1995 b/w	1993 red NO Name	1995 red No Name	1993 red WITH Name	1995 red WITH Name	1996 red WITH Name	Can b/w	Korea/China
4021	Flash													
4125	Fleece													
4012	Flip													
4118	Floppity-lavender													
4043	Flutter													
4066	Freckles													
4051	Garcia													
4023	Goldie													
4126	Gracie													
4092	Grunt													
4061	Happy-gray													
4061	Happy-lavender													
4119	Hippity-mint													
4073	Hoot													
4117	Hoppity-rose													
4060	Humphrey													
4044	Inch-felt antennae													
4044	Inch-yarn antennae													
4028	Inky-pink													
4028	Inky-tan with mouth													
4028	Inky-tan without mouth													
4082	Jolly													
4070	Kiwi													
4085	Lefty													
4020	Legs													
4057	Libearty													
4057	Libearty/Beanine													
4033	Lizzy-blue with black spots													
4033	Lizzy-tie-dyed													
4040	Lucky-7 dots													
4040	Lucky-11 dots													
4040	Lucky-21 dots													
4088	Magic-hot pink stitching													
4088	Magic-light pink stitching													
4081	Manny													
4600	Maple/Maple													
4600	Maple/Pride													
4162	Mel													

TY TAGS FILL-IN CHART

Style No	Beanie Name	Hang Tags 1st	2nd	3rd	4th	1993 b/w	1995 b/w	1993 red NO Name	1995 red No Name	1993 red WITH Name	1995 red WITH Name	1996 red WITH Name	Can b/w	Korea/China
4007	Mystic-coarse-mane													
4007	Mystic-fine-mane													
4067	Nana-tan tail													
4104	Nanook													
4003	Nip-all gold													
4003	Nip-gold/white belly													
4003	Nip-gold/white paws													
4114	Nuts													
4025	Patti-deep fuchsia													
4025	Patti-fuchsia													
4025	Patti-magenta													
4025	Patti-raspberry													
4053	Peace													
4062	Peanut-light blue													
4062	Peanut-royal blue													
4013	Peking													
4026	Pinchers													
4072	Pinky													
4161	Pouch													
4106	Pugsly													
4026	Punchers													
4024	Quacker-with wings													
4024	Quacker-without wings													
4024	Quackers-with wings													
4024	Quackers-without wings													
4091	Radar													
4086	Rex													
4086	Righty													
4014	Ringo													
4069	Roary													
4101	Rover													
4107	Scoop													
4102	Scottie													
4029	Seamore													
4080	Seaweed													
4031	Slither													
4115	Sly-brown-belly													
4115	Sly-white-belly													
4120	Snip													

Style No	Beanie Name	Hang Tags 1st	2nd	3rd	4th	1993 b/w	1995 b/w	1993 red NO Name	1995 red No Name	1993 red WITH Name	1995 red WITH Name	1996 red WITH Name	Can b/w	Korea/ China
4002	Snort													
4100	Sparky													
4030	Speedy													
4060	Spike													
4022	Splash													
4090	Spook													
4090	Spooky													
4000	Spot- with a spot													
4000	Spot-without a spot													
4005	Squealer													
4087	Steg													
4077	Sting													
4017	Stinky													
4065	Stripes-black/orange													
4065	Stripes-black/tan													
4002	Tabasco													
4031	Tank-7-line													
4031	Tank-9-line													
4031	Tank-7-line with shell													
4031	Tank-9-line with shell													
4050	Teddy-NF brown													
4052	Teddy-NF cranberry													
4057	Teddy-NF jade													
4056	Teddy-NF magenta													
4051	Teddy-NF teal													
4055	Teddy-NF violet													
4050	Teddy-OF brown													
4052	Teddy-OF cranberry													
4057	Teddy-OF jade													
4056	Teddy-OF magenta													
4051	Teddy-OF teal													
4055	Teddy-OF violet													
4042	Trap													
4076	Tuck													
4108	Tuffy													
4076	Tusk													
4068	Twigs													
4058	Valentino													

TY TAGS FILL-IN CHART

Style No	Beanie Name	Hang Tags				1993 b/w	1995 b/w	1993 red NO Name	1995 red No Name	1993 red WITH Name	1995 red WITH Name	1996 red WITH Name	Can b/w	Korea/China
		1st	2nd	3rd	4th									
4064	Velvet													
4075	Waddle													
4084	Waves													
4041	Web													
4013	Weenie													
4103	Wrinkles													
4063	Ziggy													
4004	Zip-all black													
4004	Zip-black/white belly													
4004	Zip-black/white paws													

NOTE: The embroidered cloth Ty tush tag has also been found attached to some Beanie Babies. The majority of Beanie Babies that have this tush tag have the 2nd version heart tag, as well as the Canadian tush tag. The embroidered tag is primarily used for other Ty products such as the plush line. Because of language differences and human error, this tag was accidentally attached to some Beanies when a changeover was being made from a plush product run to a Beanie Baby run.

Row 7: Twigs, Pinchers, Magic, Spike, Crunch, Congo, Mystic, Ally, Rover, Weenie, Pugsly, Legs

Row 6: Wrinkles, Scoop, Spooky, Scottie, Floppity, Hippity, Hoppity, Ears, Valentino, Curly, Maple, Teddy-brown

Row 5: Lizzy, Seaweed, Squealer, Speedy, Spot, Waves, Echo, Pinky, Doby, Tank, Velvet, Claude

Row 4: Bernie, Dotty, Patti, Waddle, Bones, Strut, Nuts, Ringo, Seamore, Bucky, Fleece

Row 3: Inky, Bessie, Daisy, Nanook, Freckles, Lucky 21, Lucky 11, Cubbie, Blackie, Roary, Goldie, Sly

Row 2: Quackers, Zip, Flip, Snip, Chip, Nip, Peanut, Pouch, Happy, Derby, Inch, Blizzard, Stripes

Row 1: Ziggy, Mel, Snort, Hoot, Chocolate, Tuffy, Baldy, Gracie, Jolly, Stinky, Bongo tan-tail, Bongo brown-tail, Peace (not shown)

Retired Beanie Babies (R)

Ally, the alligator	Grunt, the razorback hog (R)
Baldy, the eagle	Happy, the gray hippo (R)
Bernie, the St. Bernard	Happy, the lavender hippo
Bessie, the brown and white cow	Hippity, the mint green bunny
Blackie, the black bear	Hoot, the owl
Blizzard, the black and white tiger	Hoppity, the rose bunny
Bones, the brown dog	Humphrey, the camel (R)
Bongo, the monkey w/brown tail- r/w tush tag /no name (R)	Inch, the inchworm with felt antennae (R)
Bongo, the monkey w/brown tail-r/w tush tag w/name	Inch, the inchworm with yarn antennae
Bongo, the monkey w/tan tail b/w tush tag (R)	Inky, the pink octopus
Bongo, the monkey w/tan tail- r/w tush tag /no name (R)	Inky, the tan octopus with a mouth (R)
Bongo, the monkey w/tan tail-r/w tush tag w/name	Inky, the tan octopus without a mouth (R)
Bronty, the brontosaurus (R)	Jolly, the walrus
Brownie, the brown bear (R)	Kiwi, the toucan (R)
Bubbles, the black and yellow fish (R)	Lefty, the donkey with American flag (R)
Bucky, the beaver	Legs, the frog
Bumble, the bee (R)	Libearty, the white bear with American flag (R)
Caw, the crow (R)	Libearty/Beanine, the white bear with American flag (R)
Chilly, the white polar bear (R)	Lizzy, the blue lizard with black spots
Chip, the calico cat	Lizzy, the tie-dyed lizard (R)
Chocolate, the moose	Lucky, the ladybug with 7 felt dots (R)
Chops, the lamb (R)	Lucky, the ladybug with approx. 11 dots
Claude, the tie-dyed crab	Lucky, the ladybug with approx. 21 dots
Congo, the gorilla	Magic, the white dragon-hot pink stitching
Coral, the tie-dyed fish (R)	Magic, the white dragon-light pink stitching
Crunch, the shark	Manny, the manatee (R)
Cubbie, the brown bear	Maple/Maple, the white bear with Canadian flag
Curly, the brown-napped bear	Maple/Pride, the white bear with Canadian flag (R)
Daisy, the black and white cow	Mel, the koala
Derby, the coarse-mane horse	Mystic, the coarse-mane unicorn
Derby, the fine-mane horse (R)	Mystic, the fine-mane unicorn (R)
Digger, the orange crab (R)	Nana, the monkey with tan tail - b/w tush tag (R)
Digger, the red crab (R)	Nanook, the husky
Doby, the doberman	Nip, the all gold cat with pink ears (no white) (R)
Doodle, the rooster (R)	Nip, the gold cat with white face and belly (R)
Dotty, the dalmatian	Nip, the gold cat with white paws
Ears, the brown rabbit	Nuts, the squirrel
Echo, the dolphin	Patti, the deep fuchsia platypus (R)
Flash, the dolphin (R)	Patti, the fuchsia platypus
Fleece, the napped lamb	Patti, the magenta platypus (R)
Flip, the white cat	Patti, the raspberry platypus (R)
Floppity, the lavender bunny	Peace, the tie-dyed bear
Flutter, the tie-dyed butterfly (R)	Peanut, the light blue elephant
Freckles, the leopard	Peanut, the royal blue elephant (R)
Garcia, the tie-dyed bear (R)	Peking, the panda bear (R)
Goldie, the goldfish	Pinchers, the red lobster
Gracie, the swan	Pinky, the pink flamingo

	Pouch, the kangaroo			Teddy, the new face-teal bear (R)
	Pugsly, the pug			Teddy, the new face violet bear (R)
	Punchers, the red lobster (R)			Teddy, the old face-brown bear (R)
	Quacker, the duck with wings (R)			Teddy, the old face-cranberry (R)
	Quacker, the duck without wings (R)			Teddy, the old face-jade bear (R)
	Quackers, the duck with wings			Teddy, the old face-magenta bear (R)
	Quackers, the duck without wings (R)			Teddy, the old face-teal bear (R)
	Radar, the bat (R)			Teddy, the old face-violet bear (R)
	Rex, the tyrannosaurus (R)			Trap, the mouse (R)
	Righty, the elephant with American flag (R)			Tuck, the walrus (R)
	Ringo, the raccoon			Tuffy, the terrier
	Roary, the lion			Tusk, the walrus (R)
	Rover, the red dog			Twigs, the giraffe
	Scoop, the pelican			Valentino, the white bear with red heart
	Scottie, the Scottish terrier			Velvet, the panther
	Seamore, the seal			Waddle, the penguin
	Seaweed, the otter			Waves, the orca whale
	Slither, the snake (R)			Web, the spider (R)
	Sly, the brown-belly fox (R)			Weenie, the dachshund
	Sly, the white-belly fox			Wrinkles, the bulldog
	Snip, the Siamese cat			Ziggy, the zebra
	Snort, the red bull with cream paws			Zip, the all black cat with pink ears (no white) (R)
	Sparky, the dalmatian (R)			Zip, the black cat with white face and belly (R)
	Speedy, the turtle			Zip, the black cat with white paws
	Spike, the rhinoceros			
	Splash, the orca whale (R)			***ADDITIONAL BEANIES:***
	Spook, the ghost (R)			
	Spooky, the ghost			
	Spot, the black and white dog with a spot			
	Spot, the black and white dog without a spot (R)			
	Squealer, the pig			
	Steg, the stegosaurus (R)			
	Sting, the ray (R)			
	Stinky, the skunk			
	Stripes, the black and orange tiger (R)			
	Stripes, the black and tan tiger			
	Strut, the rooster			
	Tabasco, the red bull (R)			
	Tank, the 7-line armadillo (R)			
	Tank, the 9-line armadillo (R)			
	Tank, the 7-line armadillo with shell			
	Tank, the 9-line armadillo with shell			
	Teddy, the new face-brown bear			
	Teddy, the new face-cranberry bear (R)			
	Teddy, the new face-jade bear (R)			
	Teddy, the new face-magenta bear (R)			

INDEX

INDEX

Index

INDEX

INDEX

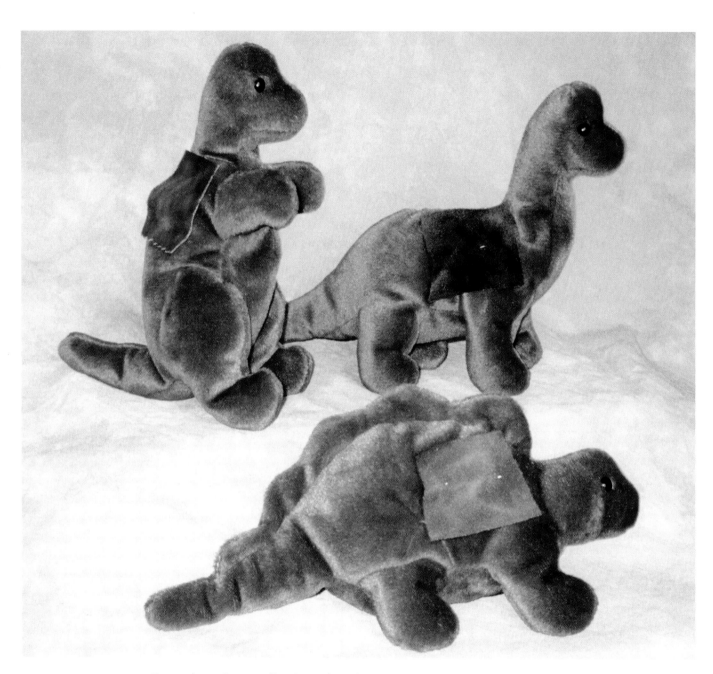

From the private collection of Becky and Becky of "Dino"mates, Inc.

Rebecca M. Phillips was born in Chicago, Illinois. She received a bachelor's degree in Education, from DePaul University and a Master's degree in Reading from Northeastern University. After 10 years, she left her passion for teaching behind to embark on a new career – motherhood. She resides in a suburb of Chicago with her husband, David, and their three children, Michelle, Michael and Caroline. In her spare time she enjoys reading, jogging and golf.

Rebecca J. Estenssoro was born in St. Louis, Missouri and raised in DeKalb, Illinois. She is a graduate of Illinois State University where she received a Bachelor of Science degree in Business Administration, with a Computer Science minor. She is a senior Application Development Analyst at a major truck manufacturing firm, located in Oakbrook Terrace, Illinois. She resides in a suburb of Chicago with her husband, Sergio, and their three children, Christopher, Audra and Matthew. In her spare time she enjoys tennis, volleyball, biking, and reading.

Rebecca Phillips and Rebecca Estenssoro write feature articles and are co-authors of the Beanie Baby "Market Analysis and Pricing Guide," for the BeanieMom website: http://www.beaniemom.com

Introductions: (Top left to bottom) Gobbles, 1997 Teddy, Snowball, Spinner and Batty

November Prices	
Ally	$15-25
Bessie	$20-35
Flip	$25-45
Hoot	$15-25
Legs	$15-25
Seamore	$50-75
Speedy	$15-25
Spot	$20-30
Tank	$30-60
Teddy	$45-75
Velvet	$15-25

Retirements: (Top left to bottom) Bessie, Flip, Velvet, Spot, Teddy Seamore, Speedy, Hoot, Tank, Legs and Ally

Beanie Mania Bulletin

by Becky Phillips

Becky Estenssoro

Vicky Krupka

Subscribe now to the **Beanie Mania Bulletin**, a newsletter updated twice a month providing you with up-to-date information on what is happening in the "World of Beanie Babies."

Included in the Bulletin will be:

❖ Updated price lists for all Beanie Babies – current, retired, redesigned.

❖ Photographs of Beanie Babies – new releases, oddities, etc.

❖ Beanie Baby news from the Internet.

❖ Answers to frequently asked questions.

❖ And much much more!

ABOUT THE AUTHORS:

In addition to being avid Beanie Baby collectors, we are regular contributors to the BeanieMom web site (www.beaniemom.com). The weekly "Price Guide" and "Netletter News" are relied upon by Beanie Baby collectors and traders all over the world. We have thoroughly researched the subject of Beanie Babies and are acknowledged experts. We have spoken on numerous radio talk shows across the country and have attended numerous collector's shows. We have had articles in various collectible magazines and our photos have been featured in TIME Magazine.

Dinomates, Inc. 710 E. Ogden Avenue, Suite 530
Naperville, IL 60563 • 1-800-247-6553

Name _____

Address _____

City_____

State _____ Zip _____

Phone_____

E-mail Address _____

_____ Six-months (12 issues) $30.00 ($36.00 Can)

_____ One-year (24 issues) $60.00 ($72.00 Can)

Thank you for your order and we know you will look forward to every issue of BEANIE MANIA BULLETIN

If ordering by mail:

Send this order form and your check, money order (US funds only) or credit card information (see below) to:

**Dinomates, Inc.
710 E. Ogden Ave., Suite 530
Naperville, IL 60563**

If ordering by fax:

Please provide credit card information in the space provided below and fax this form to (630) 357-8998.

Type of Credit Card: ☐ Visa ☐ MasterCard ☐ Discover

Credit Card #: _____

Expiration Date: _____

Signature: _____

VISA **MasterCard** **DISCOVER**